Philippe Izmailov

HOW I OVERCAME MY TRAUMA & PTSD

Self-help guide & workbook

Mindfulness Based Trauma Treatment

www.MindfulnessBasedTraumaTreatment.com

www.MindfulnessBasedTraumaTreatment.com

First print
ISBN: 978-1489504210
© 2013 Philippe Izmailov

I forgive you

Philippe

CONTENT

What's the matter with me?

It's Sunday, April 4th, Easter. Jesus has risen from his death, on the third day after his crucifixion. I have reached a deadlock in my life. I use antidepressants and I don't know how to go on with my life anymore. In a few months I'll be 33 years old.

I have reached everything I aimed at. I've got a house of my own, my education, my career, a car, a relationship. Exactly like I had in mind in my dreams. I always thought that the fulfillment of my dreams would make me happy. Why am I feeling so unhappy instead? For years and years I have worked my brains out to realize all this. Have five years of university education in Russia, four years of higher vocational education in the Netherlands, working hard in favor of my career and all the other straining efforts, all been in vain? What's the reason that my dreams failed the way they did? Could it possibly be that I have chosen my dreams the wrong way? And what's the source of all these nasty emotions which make my life so miserable? They have imprisoned me. I can't shake them off me anymore. They are the boss now. I'm doing my utmost to focus on something else, like I used to do during the past twenty years, but I'm not capable of doing this anymore at all, even if you should beat me to death! What's wrong with me?

First meeting with the psychologist

The end of June. Outside it feels sticky caused by the summer heat. On the way to my psychologist in thought I'm talking to myself. What are you going to tell her anyway? You don't remember a thing, which could be worthwhile to talk about with the psychologist! I worry about this and I feel guilty because I don't want to go spoiling her time.

On arrival I'm being welcomed by a slender woman with a short blond hairstyle, wearing a light green rather flimsy dress and she has a pleasant smile. She bears a remarkable resemblance with the front woman of the Roxette band. I wonder about her age. But that isn't a proper question to ask!, I say to myself! I take her to be a bit older than I am. I can't help thinking at once of a movie featuring a client, who's going to get an affair with her psychologist. That's not going to happen to me, isn't it? You have already found the love of your life, says a little voice inside me. Isn't she a cutie?, another little voice is asking. Come on Philippe, what do you think you're up to? You've come to this place for totally different purposes! Do you remember?

My psychologist smiles at me while giving me her hand. She introduces herself as Jennifer and asks me to take a seat. The conversation is developing very laborious. In Russia every little boy learns to become a real tough man. This means that an owner of the male sex organ is not allowed to nag, complain, cry or utter nasty feelings. In the presence of a woman he always has to behave like a "real" man. So that's what I do. Not because I want to, but because that's the way I am. Fortunately Jennifer shows a lot of patience with my "Russian masculinity". She asks me to tell her about my life. "About my life?", I ask. "Yes", she says with her soft voice. "Where you are born, how your youth went by and how you emigrated from Russia to the Netherlands.

I begin to tell her about my youth. After a short while I already reach a deadlock in my story. Like a volcanic eruption intense emotions are coming to the surface out of the dark depths of my past. I sense a furious anger and a feeling of sadness coming into my mind at the same time. I'm on the verge of bursting into tears, of which I'm not capable. Real men don't cry, as I had been teached. I don't dare to look at Jennifer. I'm terribly ashamed of my emotions. I'm staring at a light brown little coffee stain on the wall-to-wall carpeting. I'm totally stuck. I'm suddenly no longer able to say a single word. Jennifer asks me if it probably would be easier for me to put the story of my life in writing, instead of narrating it. This is what I'm going to do. I'm going home and I start with my homework. I'm going to put down for her in writing all the things which I still can remember.

During the first twenty years of my life, nearly every day was filled with a lot of stress, I felt unsafe and frequently I was overwhelmed by having fear for my life. I always kept the feelings of severe stress inside of me, because I was not allowed to complain, to get angry or to cry. I was forced to keep my emotions inside of me, otherwise I was being punished. Since I was ten years old, I began feeling depressed. I didn't want to live any more. All this can be related to the kind of upbringing my single mother treated me with. Below I describe some examples of the way I was raised.

Age 0-10 years old. Frequently outbursts of anger from my mother including violence and a lot of verbal aggression. My mother is loveless and very aloof, she doesn't acknowledge my sorrow. She is convinced that my feelings are pure nonsense and even worse, she says that they are built on figments of my imagination. I don't feel safe. I'm continuously strained. Silence in the house means a calm before the storm. I'm constantly on my guard against her aggression , outbursts of anger, blackmail or intimidations. She continuously keeps telling me that I'm a bad son and that I ruined her life. I'm feeling guilty all the time, I'm suffering from a lot of anxieties, al low self-confidence and self-esteem.

I'm a sick child. I'm frequently being hospitalized due to heart-failures, hepatitis B, influenza and other kinds of infections. I suffer from palpitations, I'm physically weak, I have a very bad head on my shoulders and I'm often tired. My mother doesn't allow me to be tired, as a result of which I have to persevere. Real men never complain, she says. I never take a break whenever I'm tired, I get across my limits. Because of my bad health during these years I'm exempted from the gymnastic lessons at school. My cardiologist has strictly ordered me to avoid any form of stress.

Age 10 years old. We move. My beloved grandmother dies. My situation has become worse. My mother is now turning sadistic. Something inside her likes to hurt me (mentally as well as physically). Every time she has maltreated me, I notice a happy satisfaction on the look of her face. She's feeling contented. Neither at home, nor outside, nor at school, I feel safe. I'm constantly being pestered both at school and in the new neighbourhood. No friends. No family. There's nobody left for me anymore. Instead I'm in the middle of a never ending war. I'm doomed to survive in a 360-degree battlefield, which is slowly choking me merciless. I have no home front or somebody who's standing beside me. I feel lonely, very sad and very depressed. These are violent hard times. I don't want to live any more. Each night, before falling asleep, I beg to God never having to wake up again. My mother isn't aware of what is going on in my terribly troubled mind. As from this age my depression is just worsening.

Age 12 till 13 years old. My mother is cooking on our veranda. An argument between us turns into a furious outburst of anger. My mother grabs a big kitchen knife and throws it at me. The knife misses my body by a few centimetres and gets stuck into the ground. Caused by shock, I'm getting totally petrified with nerves. Moreover I'm terrified and paralyzed with fear. I'm running away. After a few hours I return home, expecting my mother's anger would have been cooled down. I ask her quietly if she realizes that I could have been dead now. She looks me straight into my eyes and with her face full with hatred, she says: "I PUT YOU ON THIS WORLD AND I AM FULLY ENTITLED TO FINISH YOU OFF!" She means it and she adds that it was my fault what happened. I'm shocked by her reaction and I feel powerless and unsafe. I just can't figure it out why she hates me that much.

Age 18 years old. An unexpected outburst of anger from my mother. She suddenly grabs a hammer, raises it above my head and she attempts to hit my head with it. I grab her hands above my head and I try to protect myself. I take the hammer away from her. She regards this as a personal attack at her. "HOW DARE YOU TOUCH YOUR MOTHER!", she cries out. And her anger and aggression are increasing rapidly. I'm being beaten and I'm not allowed to defend myself. I let myself being beaten to avoid that the situation will get even worse. Her verbal aggression is still going on for a couple of days. I constantly experience a lot of stress and fear, in case she might unexpectedly do something to me.

Age 19 years old. My mother attempts to commit suicide by jumping from a railway bridge underneath a riding train. She says I'm to blame because I am a bad son. I am in a state of shock. I am paralyzed caused by a nervous breakdown and I'm terribly afraid that she is going to hurt herself some way or another. I'm suffering from a lot of stress and anxieties.

14

Age 23 years old. Caused by the immense stress because of the situation concerning my mother, I'm getting a burnout. I feel very sick, I'm continuously nauseating, strained and totally exhausted. I seriously passed my limits. I'm getting an ulcer and heart failures. One day I faint. I consult my family doctor, after which I'm being immediately hospitalized, which is going to last for a month. Afterwards I was continuously bothered by tiredness.

Age 32 years old. I'm driving on the highway at a speed of 120 kilometres an hour. On the way home I suddenly burst immensely out into tears without any reason at all. It's like rain falling down in large quantities. I don't understand what's happening to me. For years I haven't been crying and now I can't stop. As I can't see a thing in front of me because of the tears, I almost crash into the car which is driving ahead of me. I stop the car on the hard shoulder while lighting the indicators and I grant myself the opportunity to cry to my heart's content. That same day I had followed a lesson in Neuro–Linguistic Programming in Belgium, given by the famous Anne Linden, the first lady of NLP. During the break I had a short conversation with her about the love for my grandmother, after which she gave me a hug. I'll always remember Anne Linden as a warm and loving human being with a big heart.

I can't remember more than this enumeration of events. But somewhere deep inside me I know that this is just a peak of an iceberg, which rises above the surface of the water. I wonder how I would be able to get that iceberg of frozen memories out of the water and then to let it melt. Where have I stored my memories? That's what I'm going to examine!

Storage depot of memories

A remembrance is an event, an incident out of your life, stored in your memory. First the remembrance will be stored in your short term memory and afterwards it's going to relocate to your long term memory. You can compare the long term memory with the hard disk of your computer or with a library with hundreds of thousands of books (memories). When you're going through an experience in your life, this experience is being stored in the shape of an image, a sound, a touch (or a combination of these forms of expression) including the related emotional impact. In most cases you'll be able, so to speak, to recall a short movie (or an image) out of your memory, which evokes different emotions in your inner self. These emotions are part of the event. The short movie (or an image) doesn't always have to be recovered consciously. Sometimes it's happening spontaneously, when you're confronted with a certain image, a scent, a sound (like music) or with another "trigger". Like for instance a song on the radio can take you back to the past evoking a particular emotional experience. When this experience brings along pleasant emotions, we would like to experience them again and again, as a result of which the song is being played all over again. If an experience causes nasty (unpleasant) emotions, we want to avoid the replay of that song to prevent a reliving of our unpleasant feelings. So we are doing our utmost to suppress our unpleasant emotions. When common experiences are rapidly disappearing underneath the dust in the library cupboards of the long term memory, nice and nasty types during a long period are still being stored on the bulletin board of your awareness, right in front of the entrance of your library. I think this got to do with our nature. Emotion loaded memories are having priority over emotionless memories, because perhaps we have to learn something out of the first mentioned. Imagine a situation in which you are placed in an eye-to-eye confrontation with a tiger. You feel terrified. Can you see this picture in front of you? The fear connects the picture with your "hardware" (heartbeat, tension and paralysis in the muscles, adrenaline and other body functions). In this case your picture still has got another function (task). Next to image and sound, during this specific experience it has also got a function (task) of an operating system. This operating system is steering your hardware, which among other things consists of your heartbeat, your run-away speed, your level of adrenaline, your thinking skills, your concentration, your extent of sweating, etcetera. When you have managed to survive a situation like this, from now on you'll (un)consciously do anything to prevent a repetition of what happened before. And the other way around experiences with pleasurable emotions are automatically (un)consciously strived for. Why? Because nature is aware of the fact that it's especially safe for you and that this way your chances to survive are optimal. Another reason is that the feeling is simply all right! Next to image and sound, nice memories also get an operating system function.

As a matter of fact they're actually steering certain body functions. Think of excitement, heartbeat, butterflies in your stomach caused by falling in love, speed and depth of your respiration etc.

Both nice emotions and unpleasant emotions are getting a separate section in your library as well as a catalogue of their own. The sections are situated near the entrance of your consciousness, as a result of which you'll be able to fetch back the right memory very fast and effortless. This happens when asked for as well as when not asked for. The section containing unpleasant emotions is stringently guarded by yourself. After a short time already you're building a wall around it including a solid thick safe door. Nothing is allowed to come outside and you prefer not entering this section yourself either. You're hiding the key of the door somewhere in the library among the other memories. You're doing your utmost to forget the place in which you hided the key. You definitely don't want to be remembered of the existence of this section. That's why you're beginning to avoid certain things, people and experiences in your life. Because they make you feel very uneasy confronting you with memories from the nasty section. As the avoidance attempts happen to fail regularly, you'll have to keep on increasing the security of the nasty section. You're constantly improving your expertise concerning wrapping up and securing your unpleasant memories. The walls are getting thicker, the locks are getting bigger, the warning system is provided with a more complicated code. Most of the heavy emotional memories are getting a safe deposit box. The section is more and more going to look like a heavily secured safe deposit room with a lot of little safes in a bank, of which you are the sole client. You keep all safes closed. You're doing your utmost to hide, to forget and to avoid the access codes of the safes and the catalogue containing your unpleasant memories. Nevertheless after so many years this system keeps failing. Occasionally the nasty emotions escape from your heavily secured surrounding area and penetrate into your consciousness. You don't give up. The safes are loaded in containers, which then are stowed in the hold of a large container ship. You'll send the ship to sea, as far away from your conscience as possible. Later on you're going to let the ship sink in the depth of the ocean of your subconsciousness without being noticed. So your catalogue of nasty emotions also "disappears" into the depth. From that moment on you'll hardly be able to remember those nasty memories. It seems to work on your behalf, until you're getting aware of the fact that you suffer a lot from nasty emotions, which you cannot directly link to memories from the past. Suddenly the effect has lost its cause. As logic is a safe way of our thinking, our brain is going to look for a new cause. Unfortunately often beyond ourselves. As far as I'm concerned, I notice that my mind is beginning to develop new thoughts, like: "It's not my fault that I react that exaggerated! I'm not the one to blame. It's other people that make me feel that way! "

As time goes by your container ship is becoming a ghost ship, which is lying on the bottom of the sea of the subconscious. The Flying Dutchman is starting to rot. The content of the safes wants to go outside. The pressure is getting stronger and stronger. It takes more and more of your energy to keep the doors of the safes closed. Your energy consumption is increasing every year. Your Flying Dutchman keeps sailing around without being noticed in the sea of your subconsciousness.

Nasty memories are looking for a way out

Our daily awareness still has another level of consciousness, which, without being noticed, affects our
behaviour.

Your nasty memories don't exist anymore in your
consciousness. Yet regularly inexplicable things happen
which bother you. You react in an exaggerated
emotional way during your work. This disturbs your
businesslike communication and commercial relations.
You're carrying out your tasks with a two hundred
percent effort, because you're afraid being talked to
about your functioning. You avoid conflicts. You've got
an inexplicable (un)conscious fear of failure, which
causes you a lot of stress. All of a sudden you're getting
exaggeratedly angry. You burst into anger. You're afraid
to speak in front of a group of people. You're anxious
to make mistakes. You feel uncertain in particular
situations. You're afraid to bind yourself as a result of
which your relations are falling apart. You are a stress
chicken. You keep your feelings deeply hidden and you
go on acting cheerfully. You're going shopping again
because it gives you a good feeling. You're looking for
distraction by means of new experiences, consuming
and your career. You long for recognition. You want to
achieve this by means of your work. Looking good is
equal to feeling good. You spend a lot of money in
favor of your appearance (clothes, personal care, your

"image" et cetera). Your television, radio or another source of information is always switched on. You're constantly looking for distraction beyond yourself, because when silence falls on you you're beginning to feel things. Your nasty emotions are seeking to get in touch with you. They want your attention!

You continuously determine new targets during your search for "feeling good". You have a dream, an image in which you're feeling yourself the happy man you want to be in real life. This is exactly how your life should look for you to be able to feel really happy. You believe in reaching this goal. The realization of your dream can be fully completed, as soon as you have obtained a few material things like a house of your own, a good income and maybe a station car. Apart from this you also need a partner, a large kitchen, a dog, perhaps a child and surely a modest garden where you can lie down in the sun enjoying a nice drink. After having been plodding along, pushing and working your guts out for years, you're finally going to reach that goal. It precisely matches the picture which you had in mind. Everything seems all right. However there's one minor exception. It so happens that you're not feeling happy at all. You wonder what could be the reason of this and why (and especially when) things went wrong! In your mind you're going back to the past to search for events and circumstances, which gave you a good feeling at that time. You're going to hit the town, to travel, to kiss, to go motor cycling and to live a carefree life. You now start to realize that some things disappeared from

23

your life once and for all, without you having been able to say farewell to them in a decent way. They're never coming back! You feel yourself sitting behind the bars of your responsibilities. Life is more and more beginning to look like a merry-go-round. You're in the middle of it. Monday morning: the buzzing of your alarm clock, the shower, traffic lights, traffic jam, working, traffic jam, traffic lights, having dinner, watching television, going to bed. Another four days to go. At last! It's weekend! Did it really go by so fast? Another Monday morning? Year after year. School, first job, first car, first house, living together, separating, moving, living together again, traffic jams, traffic lights, holidays, children leaving home, all of a sudden you're passing the memorable age of fifty (who could ever had imagined that it would go by that fast!), then the countdown till you'll get retired begins. At last, the time has come! I'm retired! NOW I'm going to enjoy myself! At least, that's what you're thinking. The alarm clock is removed, Monday morning doesn't exist anymore, freedom at last! You call yourself lucky because you don't have cancer and you earned a good pension. But is that true? Do you really feel happy?

Influence of upbringing and neighbourhood on handling emotions

Both good and bad emotions get a special place in our upbringing and education. In general boys are told not to complain (including holding back negative emotions), while girls are teached to tell everything (including sharing emotions). Depending on your native country, you're teached to handle good and bad emotions in different ways. In the Soviet Union an average boy was being raised as a soldier, who doesn't complain, hides his pain and emotions and who is willing to sacrifice his life for his native country at all times. That's the way I was brought up: swallowing up, imprinting and especially hiding all negativity and bad emotions. A real man doesn't complain, doesn't cry and doesn't nag. Neighbourhood and culture also play an important role in the way we handle emotions. Where a Tibetan man cries with sorrow (or grief), a Russian man is drowning his sorrow in a bottle of vodka. Russian men cannot talk about their feelings until they are dead drunk. This is the secret about the alcohol abuse of Russian men. "Unfortunately" I'm one of the few Russians who isn't a heavy boozer, which is considered abnormal in the typical culture of Russian men. More than often people asked me "Are you very ill or something like it?". When, being a man in Russia, you don't drink vodka, you'll not be able to share your feelings with another person.

For the benefit of the men in Russia there are two other effective ways to express heavy emotions. Namely swearing and fighting. Both ways don't fit me. So I never had an outlet to express my emotions. Because women in Russia can share their emotions freely with each other, they consequently live longer. The average life expectance in Russia is 65 years. As for women this expectance is 71 years while for men it's only 58 years. Many men don't even reach their retirement age. My father, whom I never had a chance to get to know, was 57 years old when he died of a heart attack. Heart problems in Russia are as common as vodka.

The Russian folk psychology knows two states of consciousness, being drunk and being sober. Between these two states of mind there still is another state, which is called hangover. During the hangover state especially many sweet-and-sour gherkins are consumed. This sweet-and-sour effect quickens the return to the sober state of consciousness.

When as a Russian man you experienced traumatic events in your life and you don't drink vodka, you'll never be able to express your bad memories.

My definition of trauma

A trauma is an event in your life, which has been stored in your memory in the shape of an image or a short movie and which evokes bad emotions, thoughts and physiological reactions. I'll give you an example: at school I have been pestered by a group of youngsters. I see an image in which I'm being pestered. This arouses nasty emotions inside me. I'm feeling anger and sadness growing in my mind. I get thoughts about standing all alone facing the group. This is not fair! The image is now "steering" some physical functions inside my body. As I call it, the image now has an operating system function of my body. My heartbeat is rising, I'm feeling the tension in my muscles, my breathing is getting faster, I'm sensing the adrenaline flowing through my veins etc. In psychology my reactions to this event in my life are called "physiological reactions".

So it's not only about anger and sadness, but also about tiredness, paralysis, heartbeat, sleeping problems, lack of energy and other physical functions.

What is a commonplace event for an adult, could be traumatic for a child. Imagine a child who isn't feeling safe and isn't protected by his/her mother. Or a child who is being rejected at the very moment he/she is looking for consolation and safety with his/her parents. A minor unimportant event in the eyes of an adult, could be traumatic for a child.

A word said in a certain context, could also be (or lead to) a trauma. Try to memorize an argument during which a certain word affected you so intensely, that it made you angry and increased your heartbeat.

In this book I restrict the meaning of the word "trauma" to events which bring along nasty emotions and which most people meet on their life path. In this framework almost everybody has "a trauma".

When you run into a certain situation, your subconscious mind (your sunk "Flying Dutchman") is looking for a trauma, which can be connected (associated) with this specific situation. In that case the current situation and the trauma from the past have a common denominator, or a root or a line which connect both with each other. The trauma rapidly associates itself with the situation and goes into action in the form of nasty emotions.

An example

I get angry and I go on the defensive when I'm being criticized. Because of my anger I can't handle criticism that well. The source of my anger goes back to an incident with my mother during my childhood. I was ten years old. My mother sent me to the greengrocer. I had to buy a kilo of little red beets. The greengrocer however gave me one big red beet weighing one kilo. When I came home, my mother got very angry because she wanted little beets. First she began to scold me (criticism). Then she grabbed the net with the big beet in her hand it and she went to hit me fiercely with it. One bang hit me in my solar plexus (a place which is located a few centimeters above the navel). I laid on the ground, bended double caused by the terrible pain and I almost choked. I felt unfairness, powerlessness, sadness and anger. In my case criticism and anger are deeply connected with each other caused by this incident. When I'm being criticized nowadays, I immediately feel anger rising inside me. The anger is the instinctive reaction of Philippe.

Philippe-reaction

The Russian physiologist and winner of the Nobel prize Pavlov (1849-1936) has become world-famous with his experiments (Pavlov-reaction). He experimented with the reactions of a dog on food. Shortly before giving food to the dog, he let a bell ring. After having repeated this routine for a few times, the dog began to produce saliva as soon as he heard the bell ringing. Later on, when the dog heard the bell but didn't get food, he still produced saliva. This is caused by the fact that the brains of the dog began to associate the sound of the bell with getting food. In that way a reaction of the body (production of saliva) to a stimulus (the bell) came into being. This phenomena is called a reflex. Every evening I turn off my computer and I go outside straightaway to take my two dachshunds out for a walk. They hear the closing tune of Windows and they hurry towards the front door, because they know they are going to be taken out. Every time they hear the closing tune they're doing the same thing, even if I have not yet the intention to take them out. In other words: they associate the Windows closing tune with the time they are going to be taken out. This is a reflex. A reflex is a form of automatic response of the body to a stimulus. Think about the traffic lights. When you see the red traffic light (stimulus) while you are driving, your right foot will automatically step on the brakes (reaction).

Another similar experiment has been performed on a child by an American psychologist called Watson (1878-1958). The experiment is known as "Little Albert". The child, called Albert, was only nine months old. Watson showed a white rat to little Albert. At first he reacted unconcerned and he wasn't afraid of the rat. The experiment went on. Each time Albert saw the white rat, Watson made an unexpected loud sound behind the back of the child by striking a metallic pipe with a hammer. Albert was frightened by the loud sound and he started to cry. This way Little Albert began associating his fear of the loud sound with the sight of a white rat. This association caused that later on he got frightened of a white rat even when the loud sound wasn't there to be heard. In Neuro-Linguistic Programming (NLP) this process is known as anchoring.

This very same mechanism is hidden behind our traumas. A traumatic event doesn't need to be repeated to be able to get stored in our brains as a reflex. The reason is that a traumatic event evokes such a strong emotional (and often physical) reaction, that our brains automatically register this event as a reflex.

When someone says or does something which in our brains evokes an association with our traumas, our mind is going to react with emotions or feelings. An example: During my childhood I was often punished by my mother when I made mistakes. This caused different emotions in my body (system), among which a lot of anger. In my adult life I still react over and over again with a lot of anger if somebody is pointing at my errors. This happens just as automatically as stepping on the brakes at red traffic lights. In this example I'm well aware where the roots of my reaction come from. It's a pity that this isn't always the case. I often react unexplainable emotional in my adult life without being able to remember the underlying traumas. I call my automatic emotional reactions, which are based on my traumas from the past, my "Philippe-reactions". This way I have several and also much worse Philippe-reactions, which I try to get rid of. For instance getting overwhelmed with stress, reacting exaggerated (over-done), getting emotional, getting scared etc. These reactions are often visible and perceptible in my behaviour. They are very disturbing, for me as well as for my nearest vicinity. They have a negative influence on my communication, my work, my emotional life, my relation with my girlfriend and furthermore they lie as a grey block of concrete on the road to my happiness. I'll have to go back in time to track down my bad memories.

Mindfulness based trauma treatment

The question is: What are those bad memories, that are lying locked up in the safe-deposit boxes of the container ship? What is stored in box A? What is stored in box B? In which container could they be found? You haven't got a catalogue anymore. How can you get the traumas coming to the surface? According to the founder of the psycho analysis, the Viennese physician and psychiatrist Sigmund Freud (1856-1939) our suppressed emotions among other things reveal itself in our dreams. In your dream-sleep your sunken Flying Dutchman is coming to the surface, the pirates are opening the deposit boxes and the bad memories are regaining their freedom. The memories change clothes, perform plays, shoot movies and have a pirate party. They are now at the same time the managers, the directors and the actors of your subconsciousness. The next morning when you awake, you're hardly conscious of your dream and you go on with your life.

Great! But how could you get access to your "forgotten" container ship, when you are in a state of consciousness? While we are sleeping, our brainwaves are moving to the other frequency, the gate to your subconsciousness opens and the pirates are releasing your nasty memories. How do you reach that other frequency while you're awake? How do you manage to enter your subconsciousness? Inspired by the French neurologist Charcot (1825-1893), Freud applied hypnosis. I use a method developed by myself, which I call "Mindfulness Based Trauma Treatment" (MBTT). MBTT is based on a meditation which includes elements from mindfulness, Neuro-Linguistic programming (NLP), Buddhism and psychology. I gave this meditation the name "Trauma-meditation". Both hypnosis and meditation can bring you in "the state of mind", which will give you access to your subconsciousness.

In case of hypnosis the hypnotherapist is running the show, while in case of trauma-meditation you are behind the wheel yourself. Hypnosis functions excellently, provided that you have a good hypnotherapist. And that's going to cost you quite a lot of money. Especially in my case because of my numerous youth traumas. That was reason enough for me to develop a way of self-help technique, which I call trauma-meditation.

Everyone has his/her own impression of a meditation. It's very important that you put aside your impression for a while before you're going to start reading the next chapter.

What is trauma-meditation?

Trauma-meditation is a form of meditation which consists of four steps:

Step 1. Take-off

Step 2. Trauma-hunting

Step 3. Trauma-programming

Step 4. Trauma-paradise

Before I'm going to explain the above mentioned steps, I would gladly like to pay attention to the preparation for trauma-meditation.

Preparation for trauma-meditation

Place of meditation

To start with, you'll have to find a place in your house to be able to practice meditation. It's very important to choose a proper place. While doing so, follow your feelings instead of your common sense. Wander through your house and let your feelings make a choice! Always choose based on your feelings, even if your common sense tells you that the chosen place doesn't match the decor of the room. The place has to "feel good" and to help you to set your mind at rest and to bring you inner calmness. I advise you to use this place only for the meditations. Afterwards you'll understand why that's important. I have allowed my feelings to choose the right meditation place for me. My common sense told me the chosen place seemed to be a bit weird for the purpose, but my feelings indicated that this was the ideal place to meditate. My meditation place is on the left side of the television cupboard in my living room. When I'm meditating my face is always directed at the window, which means to the outside, to the light.

Seat

After you have chosen the place, you'll have to decide whether you're going to sit on a rug or in an easy chair. Because I've got backache, I sit in the tailor attitude in a white easy chair "Ektorp" from Ikea. It's a big soft chair, which offers me support for my back. My position isn't perfect, but I'm not eighteen anymore. I can't cross my legs anymore and my spine is being supported by the back of the chair. It doesn't matter, it isn't important! Nobody is allowed to sit on my meditation chair. Except I myself and only during my meditations.

Always-ready-to-get-in

The meditation place has to be easy accessible and an "always-ready-to-get-in" place, like a taxi which is always waiting for you outside, with a running engine and an open door. When you need to make effort to set up your meditation place each time, it could cause a huge emotional threshold when you really need to go trauma-meditating.

Now you have your own place of departure. From this place you're going to travel to your subconsciousness. Just like Amsterdam Schiphol airport, your place of departure should always be a "ready-to-go" place.

Step 1. Take-off

Have you ever traveled by airplane? The take-off is the moment when an airplane is leaving the ground and enters the sky. This should be the first phase of your trauma meditation.

Purpose of the take-off

The purpose of a take-off is bringing yourself in a "state of mind" by which you can get access to your subconsciousness. This state of mind is nothing else but a light sleep in a state of still being conscious.

Our sleep has four phases. In the first phase we are falling lightly asleep (slumbering, drowsing). Our consciousness is decreasing. Our brain waves are moving from the awake condition (8-12Hz) to the light sleep condition (4-7Hz). In the second phase you're completely losing your consciousness (12-16Hz). In the third phase you're falling into a deep sleep (1-3Hz). In the fourth phase, which is called the REM sleep, you're starting to dream (4-12Hz). This is the phase when our Flying Dutchman (including his bad memories) comes to the surface. The brain waves in this phase (4-12Hz) have a big overlap with the light sleep (4-7Hz). From my own experience I can say that in both sleeping phases our suppressed memories are liable to come to the surface.

So the purpose of the take-off is nothing else than having your brain waves lowered in order to get access to your Flying Dutchman. Or simply said, you'll have to allow yourself to doze away but at the same time you'll have to stay conscious. You do this every day when you're falling asleep. So it's a question of practicing a little bit.

In case of many people the first sleeping phase only lasts a few minutes. Next you're going into the second sleeping phase and you lose your consciousness. The challenge is to prevent yourself from going into sleeping phase two and to stay conscious. This is necessary because you'll need your consciousness to be able to perform the trauma meditation. How do you start your take-off? Follow the take-off procedure.

Take-off procedure

Just like a pilot who is going through a number of prescribed steps before getting airborne, we are also going to pass through some steps

Stap 1. Have a comfortable seat

Your position during the trauma meditation should be consistent with a fixed rule. Find a position in which you feel yourself physically well and especially relaxed. It doesn't matter which position you're exactly going to take, as long as it does not hinder you during the meditation. Your position should not distract you and certainly must not disturb you! When I intend to sit down with a 100% straight back, my attention will almost totally be aimed at keeping my back 100% straight instead of being focused on the meditation. Please sit down comfortably and close your eyes.

Step 2. Concentrate yourself on your breathing

The next step in our take-off procedure is your breathing. Concentrate yourself on your breathing. The concentrating should be relaxed. Simply follow your breathing. Your attention is just like a human being who is going up and down with the elevator (breath). This is one of the basic techniques of the Buddhist meditation. At first you will notice that our restless human mind is constantly firing off new thoughts. "What am I going to eat tonight? Do I have enough food for the weekend? How do I solve my problems? Oh, I urgently have to do something, which I really cannot afford to forget!". And so on and so on. Before you know you'll be dragged along with the stream of thoughts, searching for answers and solutions. This way a quarter of an hour has passed and you are still even farther away from your original target.

The stream of thoughts is characteristic for the human mind. The trick is not to try to shove the thoughts away, but instead not to draw attention to them. Thoughts are like yellow leaves, which in the autumn are floating down the river following the stream. When you pick up a leaf, you pay your attention to that particular leaf, whereas your attention should stay concentrated on your breathing. This way you float along with the stream from one leaf to another. In that manner you are being automatically dragged along with the stream of thoughts. When you just stay at the side of the river as an observer, after a while your thoughts are going to disappear by themselves. Don't pay attention to every single leaf. Look at the whole, look how the leaves are slowly floating away.

How do you keep being an observer? You remain an observer when you direct your full attention exclusively at your breathing (the way you breath).Your attention should not anymore be directed at several other things, but only at one purpose and that should be the way you're breathing. Let your thoughts be slowly floating away like clouds in the sky.

Step 3. Let your mind fall into a light sleep

How do you manage to fall into a light sleep? You relax your mind, put your thoughts aside and let the substances in your brains do the job. The substance that causes us to fall asleep, is called melatonin. Melatonin is an hormone. This natural sleeping pill is activated by the epiphysis (pineal gland) in our brains when it's getting dark. This is one of the reasons why the trauma meditation takes place with our eyes closed. When I'm falling asleep, I'm sensing a nice relaxed feeling in my head, which is going to pull me into the sleeping stage. That feeling is caused by the melatonin.

Tip! Study your own falling asleep procedure. This will help you to get through this step.

When your mind is deeply relaxed and free of thoughts, like in case of the light sleep, you're ready for the trauma-hunting.

Step 2. Trauma-hunting

Before I'm going to explain what's the meaning of trauma-hunting, I would like to spend a few words on our emotions. How are emotions evoked in our minds?

Playing emotions

What do I understand by emotions in this book? An emotion is a reaction of our brains on a certain event. You know what emotions are. Don't you? So I don't need to mention examples.

Do you still remember the ancient jukebox from the good old times of Elvis Presley? It's a big, coin operated, stereo record player, which contains a series of long playing records (LP's) and a mechanism to select these records. In the belly of the jukebox you will find several LP's, which are vertically positioned in a circle on a round platter. There is also a grab arm hanging to lift up and put down the LP's . When you have chosen a song, the regarding LP is picked up by the grab arm and is placed down on the turntable. Then the song is being played. In the same manner as our emotions are being played.

Everybody has got a stock of emotions. We all know emotions like envy, anxiety, remorse, admiration, joy, hate, hope, jealousy, love, disdain, shame, feeling of guilt, regret, pride, sadness, boredom, reproach, desperation and anger, each of which is separately stored within us like an LP. These emotions can be evoked by certain events or actions during our life. When someone pushes a certain button on me, the grab arm will select the LP "anger" and let it play. In case of someone else, this button could be associated with another LP, for instance "envy". The difference in the association is caused by personal experiences, which serve as background for these emotions. The button is being pushed by an external trigger, which evokes an (emotional) reaction. Among other things it could be a sound, an image, a smell, a touch, someone's behaviour or an expression. An example. I had a colleague who was behaving disrespectful and disdainful. Caused by this (consequently) he made me play the LP "anger". I know that at that very moment on my other colleague's jukebox the LP "envy" was being played.

Another example. When I hear wailing sirens of ambulances, I start getting nice emotions. These emotions came into being during my holiday in Paris. I was lying on the bed in my hotel room while the window was open, enjoying the sounds of the city (among other things sirens) and I felt happy. My former neighbor on the other hand suffers from very heavy emotions when hearing the same sirens. Her husband died in an ambulance on his way to a hospital. So it's completely understandable that the emotions we felt when hearing the sound of the sirens, were totally each other's opposite.

Mechanism of associating emotions with events

How does the jukebox know which LP associates with which button? This information has been programmed somewhere on the printed circuit board of the jukebox. On this board a button is being linked to an emotion. In our brains this function has a special domain, which is called the limbic system.

The limbic system among other things consists of the brain domains the amygdala and the hippocampus. The amygdala lays connections between information from our senses and couples these with emotions. The emotional information processing takes place in the amygdala, among which the observation of danger as well as the experience of fears. The hippocampus then gives meaning to that observation. In other words: the limbic system is steering our jukebox, is letting the grab arm taking the right LP and is letting it play.

Reprogramming the jukebox

Hardware

OK, let's have a quick look under the hood of our jukebox. What do we see? Buttons, threads, Lp's and a play mechanism. Let's go see what is going to happen in my jukebox when I hear a siren. When the "siren" button is pushed, the electric signal is going to the LP "happiness" and then this LP is being played. The LP and the button are linked to each other with a blue thread. When we cut this thread, my button "siren" will be disconnected from the LP "happiness". In other words I'm not going to feel happiness anymore when I hear the siren. On the other hand the button of my former neighbor will be connected by the red thread to the LP "sadness".

As you will understand, we cannot open the skull of my former neighbor to cut off the correct red thread. Anyhow, that isn't necessary. There is another way to solve this problem. We can cause the red thread to be burned through. To be able to do this, we'll have to overstrain the thread. How are we going to manage this? We are going to evoke a very strong positive emotion during the reliving of a trauma. Then the nasty emotion together with the positive emotion has to cause an overstrain in the thread. Let me try to explain this otherwise. As long as I use my garden hose by means of an ordinary tap, this hose will stay intact. When I connect my garden hose to the local fire fighters crane, I will certainly end up with a burst garden hose. How is this caused? The water pressure in the fire fighters crane is that high, that my garden hose definitely is going to burst. In the same way we can cause an enormous pressure in the red thread, as a result of which it will be burned through.

My neuropsychological theory

What exactly is the meaning of the thread? In this section I'll try to give my own semi-scientific explanation. I'll keep it as simple as possible. My LP "Anger" has been linked to the button by the thread. In our brains these kind of threads are called neural networks. A thread consists of a sequence of neurons. The neurons are not joined to each other. The spaces between the neurons are called synapses. The neurons communicate with each other by passing on a message (signal), so-called neurotransmitter (just like two people sending emails to each other). A neurotransmitter is a signal material which delegates impulses between neurons. If the neurons are not joined to each other, how is it possible that they become one thread? The neurons will not become one thread until a neurotransmitter "connects" the neurons to each other. Put ten coins on the table in one straight line with a difference of half a centimeter between each other. That should be ten neurons. At this moment they are not yet linked to each other. Take a watering can and let some drops of water (neurotransmitters) fall between all these coins, so the water will eventually connect all coins to each other. Now these coins are making up one thread. So through this thread an electric signal can be passed now.

Emotions can make the thread stronger or weaker caused by additional neurotransmitters, which are coming free (being released). I think that every emotion knows its own neurotransmitter and/or a combination of different neurotransmitters. In other words: my anger and my love do both have their own neurotransmitter(s). When I replace the neurotransmitters of anger by the neurotransmitters of love, the original thread in my jukebox will be dissolved. A new thread with the neurotransmitters of "Love" could arise. When I evoke a very strong positive emotion during the reliving of my trauma, my thread will get overloaded with additional neurotransmitter(s). These neurotransmitter(s) belong to the positive emotion. The strain leads to annulment of the original thread and sometimes to the development of a new thread with another neurotransmitter. Evoking the right neurotransmitter is the key to success in the process of trauma reprogramming.

For example, let's take two different neurotransmitters, namely dopamine and adrenaline. Dopamine provides delight, an extremely pleasant feeling for a human being. Adrenaline is produced in case of fear, stress, anger, cold, heat and pain. In my case dopamine is activated when I hear a siren. On the other hand, in case of my former neighbor the adrenaline is being increased when she's hearing the same sound. Imagine that I would be able to exchange my dopamine with my former neighbor for adrenaline. What would I be going to feel? In any case I'm not going to be capable of experiencing feelings of happiness any more.

During the reliving of my trauma I create an action or an act which evokes a positive emotion in my mind. The emotion has to be a lot stronger and the opposite of the nasty emotion. This emotion will evoke another (other) neurotransmitter(s), which eventually is (are) going to banish the original neurotransmitter(s). This is going to cause the overstrain and the annulment of the original thread. For this reason the button of the LP will be disconnected. This way I manage to get rid of my nasty emotions. In some cases the nasty emotion will even be replaced by an opposite strong emotion. I'll take an example of a youth trauma, caused by bullying carried out by a group of youngsters at school. Some of the original nasty emotions consisted of my uncertainty and my powerlessness. Everybody could notice this in my behaviour. I have treated this youth trauma during a trauma-meditation. When nowadays I think back to this bullying, I feel a lot more self-confidence as well as a tremendous power. If someone should start bullying me now, he/she would get a very firm reaction from me in return.

Software

Our jukebox also has a volume button, which adjusts the sound intensity of the LP. The same LP can be played loudly or softly. When the volume button is tuned on "max", the sound will come out of the juke-box at its loudest. Let's observe my example when my LP "anger" had been evoked by my colleague and was played by my jukebox. My anger was not that intense, that I would have going to beat my colleague. There is a difference in the intensity of emotionality. On a scale from 0 to 10, I would give my anger a 7. 0 stands for the minimal volume, while 10 stands for the maximal volume. Let's say that in case of a 10, I would have gotten so angry, that I most likely would have hit my colleague, while in case of a 0 I wouldn't have felt any anger at all. This intensity is nothing else than the volume level of our LP.

The same LP "anger" can be played in different situations with a different volume level. In another situation than in the one with my colleague, my LP "anger" could be played with the volume level 4. Every LP in our jukebox has its own unique code. The code is being derived from the first two letters of the involved emotion. The LP "anger" has a code AN, the LP "fear" has a code FE et cetera. When you add the volume level to these codes, you get the complete programming code, like FE7 or FE4. In the example with my colleague, he has evoked in my jukebox an automatic Philippe-reaction AN7. This means that my LP anger"(AN) had been played with volume level 7.

How would I be able to make my AN7-code so little, that it becomes AN(0)? Or how would I be able to replace my AN7 by another emotion? Behind most of the Philippe-reactions there is a trauma, which each time associates itself with the current situation. That's where the emotion AN7 comes from. In the perception of Little Albert the experiment of Watson was a traumatic experience. When we successfully change the emotional perception of a traumatical experience from the past, we also change automatically our emotional reaction in the present. If Little Albert wouldn't have been confronted with loud noises, he wouldn't have been scared and therefore he wouldn't be afraid of the white rats. How can I change the emotional perception of my traumatic experience? During the reliving of my trauma I'm going to evoke a very strong (positive) emotion.

Before we can change our traumatic experience from the past, first we'll have to be able to call that experience back to our mind. In my case this was not possible any more. I couldn't remember my traumatic experiences any more. That's why I had to track down my sunken Flying Dutchman with its safe deposit boxes.

We are going back in time looking for that traumatic experience, which is responsible for the emotional reaction. I called this search operation a trauma-hunting.

Method of trauma-hunting

The hunting season has been opened. We're going hunting for our trauma's from the past. Do you still know where they could be found? The traumas are locked up in the safety deposit boxes of the Flying Dutchman, which is sunk somewhere on an unknown spot in the deep ocean of our subconsciousness. How are we going to recover the Flying Dutchman? How are we going to hunt for our traumas ? It's like hunting for mice. You don't know where they are hiding, but they can't resist to show up to get a piece of cheese. Like most ships our Flying Dutchman also has mice who are hiding in the safe-deposit boxes. We are going to hunt for these mice (traumas). Have you never caught mice? Here is my instruction. Put down a mousetrap with some bait in it and keep waiting.

Let's observe that particular example of the incident with my colleague. Caused by his behaviour I felt anger coming up. Somewhere in my jukebox the LP "anger" is associated with a particular trauma. This association has an analogy with Freud's method of free association.

My feeling of anger is my bait. The trauma- meditation is like a mouse trap into which the mouse (the trauma) is going to enter. In my sleep my jukebox is capable to track down the right trauma, that is to say the trauma, which evokes my anger. The same result can be achieved during the trauma-meditation. I think that now the time has come to start with a bit of practicing.

Script of a trauma-meditation (steps 1 and 2)

1. Take-off. Sinking into the depth of the sea of the subconsciousness.

Before starting the trauma-meditation you'll have to study the take-off procedure of this meditation. Sit down. Imagine you're in the cockpit of a modern fighter jet plane. You're totally safe. You're breathing slowly and deeply through an oxygen mask from the supply in your respiration device. You ought to concentrate on your breathing. Wait until you're relaxed and your head has calmed down. This brings your brainwaves in the frequency, which is comparable to the light sleep. This is very important! If you're not sufficiently "submerged" into your meditation, the Flying Dutchman will not come to the surface and your traumas will not come into your consciousness. A mouse is not going to be captured as long as it's constantly busy around the mousetrap (caused by the presence of restless thoughts, tensions etc.).

2. Trauma-hunting. Setting mousetrap

Now you should call up a recent event, which evokes a typical "Philippe reaction" in your mind. In my case it was my anger, which was evoked by my colleague. You're still sitting safely in the cockpit. The experience which you have evoked, has brought along an emotion. Determine in which part of your body this emotion has settled itself. Release yourself from your recent experience. Make this experience disappear. Just leave the emotion behind. Don't you worry if this will not succeed. In this case it's the emotion that counts. This is what we need right now. Draw your attention to the spot where the emotion is anchored in your body. Concentrate yourself on this spot and wait. The mousetrap has been set up. Now you'll have to keep waiting.

The emotion on which you're concentrating yourself is reflected in the visor of your fighter jet. You have got a target in your visor That's why I call this emotion a target-feeling. This is the bait with the help of which we're going to lure a mouse out of our Flying

Dutchman. What will happen after the waiting? When you have sufficiently been "sunk" into the meditation, you will get a traumatic event from the past showing up in your mind. This traumatic event is responsible for the origin of your emotion. Your jukebox has associated this traumatic event with your "Philippe-reaction".

* N.B. When you haven't got a recent event at your disposal, but you are nevertheless bothered by emotion (or a feeling) you should concentrate yourself directly on that emotion (the target-feeling). Further down in this book you'll find examples of that kind of meditations.

Example of a trauma-meditation

I refer to the earlier mentioned situation with my colleague. He is behaving himself disrespectful and disdainful. This has a certain effect on me (a button of my jukebox is being pushed in). His behaviour arouses strong feelings of anger in me (AN7). Caused by the anger, I cannot get a single word out of my mouth anymore when I try to talk to him about his conduct. I can hardly give him a slap on the face to express my anger. My emotions bother me a lot. I haven't the faintest idea why I'm experiencing this much of anger and what's the source of this. I want to get rid of it.

I'm going to sit in my meditation chair. I see to it that my head is relaxed and I recall the experience.

Target-feeling

My target-feeling is my feeling of anger. It's somewhere in my breast. I'm concentrating on it and I wait.

Trauma-experience

An image is appearing. I'm seeing myself in secondary school. I'm being surrounded by a group of older youngsters. One of them is about a heads length shorter than his peers. They are much older than I am. I'm being pestered and belittled by him and by his friends. There is no way out. I'm going to lose the battle against the group. I can't stand up for myself. I'm furious and I feel powerless.

My jukebox links my anger from the event in secondary school to the incident with my colleague. In both situations I couldn't hit either the bully nor my colleague. I experienced a lot of anger which was desperately looking for a way out.

OK, you tracked down the right trauma, which is responsible for your "Philippe-reaction". What now? (What 's the next step?).

Step 3. Trauma-programming

We have caught a mouse now. What are we going to do with it? Now I know the origin of my anger in the situation with my colleague. It was caused by an incident at the secondary school. I can't change this incident. It happened in my past. But on the other hand I can change the experience of this event in my memory. The purpose of this change is to unchain my emotional reaction from the event. In other words: I'm going to separate my anger from my recollection. An example. When I think back to the incident at the secondary school, I don't want to feel anger but instead I strive to get a feeling of a lot of strength and confidence. My jukebox is especially going to associate my strength and confidence with the incident with my colleague. This will enable me to use my strength and confidence when I'm talking to the person in question about his/her behavior the next time. I shall not feel anger standing in my way anymore. How will I be able to reach this goal?

Our life is like a movie which lasts decades. All life events are recorded on a filmstrip, which can be played later on by a filmstrip projector in our head (reminding memories). When a certain event evokes a strong emotion within us, the filmstrip in the projector is getting jammed which results in a replay of the same fragment on the screen over and over again*. In the filmstrip projector arises an overstrain. At that moment the event including the corresponding emotion will be stored in the memory of our jukebox.

In the future the jukebox will be looking for a similar life event and will put on the same LP "emotions", which is associated with the jammed filmstrip. We are going to repair that jammed piece of the filmstrip, so that the movie can be resumed.

NB:* In the worst case (scenario) you're going to develop Posttraumatic stress disorder (like I did) as a result of which you'll be reliving the very same traumatic event over and over again.

According to the Accelerated Information Processing Model of the American psychologist Francine Shapiro, (who developed the EMDR-therapy) trauma is causing changes in neurotransmitters as well as in en adrenaline, which then are causing a "lack of balance" in the nervous system. The handling of information is being blocked (the filmstrip in the projector is getting jammed). The brains as well as the rest of the body are getting dislocated and are consequently not being able anymore to perform the way they should be. The painful memories are frequently being triggered by a variety of internal and external stimuli. This appears in shapes of flashbacks, nightmares, relivings and arousals. In case of a well-functioning "Information Processing

System", there exists a neurological balance in the information-processing (as a result of which the filmstrip in the projector is not getting jammed).

Let's take a close look at that jammed piece of the movie. I'm going to relive the trauma to be able to understand what kind of emotion that experience is calling up (evoking) in me. I'm being pestered and belittled by a boy together with his friends. That arouses an anger within me, which I cannot express (utter), because together with his friends he has a dominate position. Uttering that feeling of anger is very important for me at that particular moment. But I can't. That's the reason why my anger, by means of a piece of jammed filmstrip, is automatically being stored by my jukebox. So I'll have to return to the experience to be able to utter my anger. This is perfectly possible during the trauma-meditation and it's completely safe for myself as well as for the vicinity (the people around me).

NB: In this book I'm using three different names to call myself. "Little Filipp" (age till 10 years old), Filipp (age 10 till 20 years old) and Philippe (age between 20 years old and now).

My trauma-meditation goes on.

I'm seeing myself (Filipp) standing before a group of about twelve youngsters. They have surrounded (besieged) him. They're spitting on him, kicking him with their feet and pushing him in his back. They're having a great time.

I intervene. I draw a thick glass wall between Filipp and those youngsters. I go to Filipp and I ask him how I could be able to help him. What do you need at THIS VERY MOMENT?, I ask him. He wants a pair of boxing gloves. He asks me to separate the group from the leader, so he can grind an axe with the leader only. Filipp gets everything he wants at this very moment. I draw the glass wall over him and the leader of the group. They are now standing in the middle of it. The rest of the group has gathered behind the glass wall and is waiting for the things to come. Filipp beats up the tormentor and asks me to open up the wall. I do what he wants. Then he starts beating up everyone, who's near to him. Especially the ones, who had been pestering him most of all. Most of them are lying on the ground in no time. The others ran away. The ones on the ground don't have the guts to fight against Filipp. They're crawling away. It's a wonderful feeling to be able to let your anger come out of your system and moreover to be able to stand up for yourself. Filipp gets a feeling of self-confidence. He's feeling strong enough to stand up for himself. He also feels ME (the grown up Philipp) standing behind him. Knowing that he isn't alone at the enemy front, surely gives him a secure feeling.

At last my Philippe-reaction in similar situations has been changed from anger to self-confidence. In this example I reward my self-confidence with an 8-grade. My jukebox is being updated automatically. From now on it plays the LP "Self-confidence" with a volume of 8 instead of the LP "Anger" with a volume of 7 in a similar situation like the incident with my colleague. The programming code AN7 has been replaced by SE8.

Programming emotions

Are you familiar with the internet? If so, you surely have been confronted with a web page. A web page consists of images and texts, which are providing the visitor with a total view in a specific layout. Behind that view is a programming code, which is called the source code. Do you want to see this code? Look for a submenu "the source code" or "the page source" in the main menu of your browser and you're going to see a page with numbers and letters. This is the programming code of the web page.

In the same way the source code of our emotions is hidden behind the image of our recollection. Or explained otherwise: Behind our recollection (web page) a source code is hidden (for instance AN7), which maintains an emotional experience of our recollection in our memory (the browser). The web page and the source code are inextricably linked to each other.

If you change the source code, you'll automatically change the web page. Previously a programmer had to change the source code himself to be able to change the web page. He had to understand the meaning of the digits and the letters behind the web page. Nowadays a special software program (HTML editor) is used for this purpose. By means of this program you'll be able to directly change the web page yourself. You don't need to understand the source code. After having changed the web page, the source code will be also automatically changed. This is the thought (idea) behind my trauma-programming. When you change the image (movie) of your recollection you automatically change your emotional experience of the recollection (for instance the source code can be changed from AN7 to SE8).

You'll understand that it's hard for me to actually express my bottled up (hoarded up) anger. It's nearly impossible to go and beat up the youngsters in my example to still take my revenge, even if I could track them down after more than twenty years. As a matter of fact this isn't necessary at all. The point is, that you are emotionally being able to redress (or heal) the traumatic experience in your recollection". It doesn't matter that you're experiencing self-made-up events during the trauma programming, which never took place in your

61

past. The question is: Does it work for you or doesn't it? From my experience I can say this: After a healing of my traumatic recollections in the trauma-meditation, my memory would be changed (reprogrammed). My adjusted recollection with self-made-up events and new emotional response (or experience) would be stored in my memory instead of the former one. When I think back to the recollection with that group of youngsters, I feel self-confidence and power instead of anger and powerlessness. I feel the same with regard to situations at present, when a person is behaving disrespectful and disparaged. So the trauma-programming is permanent. I think that a lot of little children are "redressing" (or healing) their traumatic experiences in the same way in order to get rid of their nasty emotions. They are going to relive the experience where they were saying and doing things, which gave them a good feeling. Sometimes they are doing this during their playing. In that way they are letting out their jammed emotions. They are doing this by themselves. In my opinion this is anchored in human nature.

Who's doing what in the process of trauma-meditation?

There are always two persons involved in the (same) trauma-meditation. I myself am both of them during two different periods. An adult from the present who is pulling the strings and his counterpart from the traumatic experience in the past. As a matter of fact you're wearing two caps. You play the role of both the practitioner and the client, of both the flight instructor and the apprentice, of both the director and the actor. It's the same combination as mother and daughter. You have a daughter but at the same time you also have your own mother. You are a mother as well as a daughter at the same time. You can experience your own feelings as a mother and as a daughter at the same time.

Keep your distance from your emotions.

During the trauma-meditation I experience the difference between the emotions of Filipp from the trauma-period and of the emotions of Philippe in the present. I then feel emotions which belong to Filipp from the past and I feel emotions which belong to Philippe from the present. The emotions of Filipp from the past have to be treated. They can be so overwhelming and compelling that I can't separate myself from the emotions. I'll have to be able to keep distance from those nasty emotions to make them manageable. In other words: I must disconnect (separate) myself from my horrible emotions. I'll have to keep myself thinking rationally at all times, without being carried away with my emotions. This is necessary for the role of Philippe from the present in the trauma-meditation. How am I going to manage that? I'm often seeing myself in a traumatic experience from the past. This looks like a movie with Filipp playing a leading part in it. When I see him I feel his emotions coming up into my mind. I try to feel them without directly associating them with Philippe of the present. How do I manage this? An example: In the same way I'm watching a movie in a cinema. I see an actor in an emotional scene. His girlfriend is dying. I'm feeling his grief. I say to myself: "It isn't my sorrow, it's his sorrow". I'm not the grief. I sense the boundary between "I am" and my emotion. I am not my emotion. This belongs to me just like my nose, my eyes, my ears, my legs and my hair also belong to me. That way I can feel the grief of the actor and at the same time I'm able to keep thinking rational without being carried away by his overwhelming emotions. Thinking rationally is part of the role practiced by the Philippe of the present. Because he is the one who's guiding me through my trauma-meditations. His emotional state of mind always has to remain neutral, independent and impartial. "But how are you going to manage this? ", one could ask. I'm able to handle this by not feeling sorry for myself. It's very important for the benefit of the trauma-meditation that you don't feel sorry for yourself. When I feel sorry for myself, I turn automatically into the role of the victim. Therefore I wouldn't be able to experience my emotions separated from my mind and I would completely getting jammed in my trauma-meditation. My advice is: develop compassion for yourself instead of feeling sorry for yourself. Compassion is not Self-Love, but it's love with (for) yourself. It's definitely not selfishness. Feeling sorry for yourself is destructive. It's pulling you towards the bottom of the pit. Having compassion for yourself is healing, it pushes you up to heaven, to the sun. How are you going to get rid of your self-pity? Examine your thoughts. Somewhere there has to be a way of thinking, like: " Look what they have done to me!... I'm the victim of .... It's not my fault.... I had bad luck with ... It's my fate that... That's only happening to me! She's the lucky one and I'm not! That kind of thoughts are an inexhaustible source of self-pity. At a certain point I understood that this would hardly take me anywhere. I said to myself: Yes, I had a traumatic youth, which is still standing in my way. How can I possibly manage to redress (or heal) my trauma, so that I can leave this period behind me at last? I want to make something positive out of the rest of my life (I'm 34 years old while I'm writing this book). How can I still enjoy my life? How can I be happy? All this should be considered to be my fuel for preparing and starting up my trauma-meditation.

Below follows a script which you can use to unleash your bad emotions from your traumas.

Script of trauma-meditation (step 3)

3. Trauma-programming

Start with the meditation. You went through the take-off and the steps for trauma-hunting. You have been sinking into the sea of subconsciousness. You have been setting up a mousetrap and you have been catching a mouse. You now have an image, a trauma from your past. Distance yourself (take distance) from your emotions.

You see an image or a movie showing a trauma. Start distancing yourself from your emotions. See yourself on a large cinema screen. You're sitting in the cinema room. You're looking at the movie and you see yourself performing in it. You see yourself in the traumatic experience. Don't you feel sorry for yourself. Take care that you're not getting overwhelmed with your emotions. Say to yourself: "I'm not my emotions!" "I'm not my fears!". Release yourself from your emotions. If this might not going to succeed (for the time being) because your experience is so overwhelming and/or you're being carried away with your emotions as a result of which you're getting completely jammed, then use the mechanism of the trauma-catapult from the chapter "Do's en don'ts of trauma-meditation". The trauma-catapult is going to get you out of the traumatic experience. It's important that you're able to keep thinking rationally during your trauma-meditation. Think of two roles, respectively the role of a flying instructor and the role of an apprentice (trainee). The flying instructor gives instructions to his trainee, helping and supporting him, watching him, communicating with him, taking care that the flight is going safely, intervening when necessary, pulling (if needed) the handle of the catapult mechanism, et cetera.

Relive your trauma

Let the image or the movie get through to you properly. Don't push it away out of your mind. Go through the traumatic experience fully (completely) till the end. Determine the emotions which the experience arouses in you. These emotions belong to the trainee.

What does the trainee need?

Feel his emotions. Ask your trainee what he needs in this situation. What does he need to express his nasty emotion? What does he need to get a strong positive emotion? When he's very young (for example a kid of five years old) you can sense it by yourself. Usually it comes down to comforting, providing safety, affection and a lot of love.

Change your image (movie)

Change the situation in your image (movie) as a result of which your trainee will get the emotions he needs. These emotions are the opposite of the emotions which are troubling him. How do you change the movie? You can do this by adding a new action or a new element to your movie. Use your creative ability, your fantasy. Drop the boundaries of reality. In your movie everything is possible. Study the chapter Do's en Don'ts of the trauma-meditation.

Action

Think of a new action or a new act in your movie, which evokes the required emotions in your trainee. This action can be performed by you or by your trainee or by both. Think of the boxing gloves, which were given to Filipp to be able to beat up his abusers.

Element

You can also add a new element to the movie. Think of the glass wall, which separated the group of youngsters in the above mentioned example. This element has brought Filipp to safety so that he could switch to using action. Apart from that you can change the following elements in your movie:

- ➤ Lighting. Put more light into the image. For example the sunlight. Feel the effect on the emotions of your trainee. This has a very good influence on me during my trauma-meditations.

- ➤ Colors. You can make the colors softer or just more intense. Or for example you can make the image turn into black and white or the other way around.

- ➤ The size of or the distance to the image. You can enlarge or reduce the image itself or the distance to the image.

> Velocity of playing. Let the movie play faster or slower.

> Sounds. Make them softer or louder. Replace current sounds by new or familiar sounds. Introduce new sounds. Change voices of persons. For instance let someone talk with the voice (intonation) of Mickey Mouse etc.

> Scents. Change scents. Introduce new or already familiar scents.

> Tangible elements. For instance let the warm sea breeze blow into your face.

When you're going to introduce a new element, you'll have to carefully empathize what could be the influence on the emotion of your trainee. Is it going to help? Or isn't it going to help? If the answer is negative, you should try to apply another element.

Emotion check

Let your new action and element do their job. Check if the bad emotions of your trainee are beginning to diminish. Your goal is to minimize the strength of your bad emotions (almost) to a zero level. Continue until your nasty emotions are (almost) being replaced by opposite emotions. Do you still remember my example concerning that "mob" of youngsters? The programming code AN7 in my case has been replaced by SE8. When you sense that the desired effect has not been realized, you should try to invent a new action and/or a new element. At the end of the trauma-programming, you'll take your trainee to a trauma-paradise.

Step 4. Trauma-paradise

In my emotional world I have created a virtual place filled with unconditional love and blissful happiness. I made up this paradise all by myself. It only exists in my memory (imagination capability). When I close my eyes, I see a warm waterfall with a blue lake, surrounded by green covered mountains and tropical trees. In this place the sun is always shining. It's not too hot and neither too cold. I hear the sound of the waterfall and of the colorful tropical birds. I feel the soft warm breeze in my face and the cool water splashing which refreshes the air. It's delicious to be there. The trauma-paradise is never being visited by strangers. It's a forgotten place in the middle of a tropical jungle.

After the trauma-programming my trainees go to the trauma-paradise. Like war veterans they are sent there to regain relaxation, inner rest and joy. After arriving they are being taken care of by the most loving human being which has ever been in my life. That's my grandmother. She grants her love and consolation to every trainee who arrives there. The trauma-paradise is a very important step in the trauma-meditation. With this step you're rounding off your trauma-programming.

What's the purpose of this step? When you have changed your webpage, you obviously want to save the alterations. You do this by pressing the button "save as", then by choosing a place to save (for instance the "My documents folder") and then finally by saving the web page in this folder. I use the same mechanism for the trauma-programming. I save the programming-code (SE8) in my trauma-paradise.

Invent your own trauma-paradise. It doesn't matter what it is and where it is. The main thing is, that you're feeling safe and happy while being there. Use your creative ability. Also imagine someone, who's going to play the role of my grandmother in your trauma-paradise. He or she is going to take care of your traumatized trainees and to give them love, affection and warmth. This could be a deceased family member or a beloved one who's still alive. The role of my grandmother is very essential in the trauma-paradise. Once you have experienced this yourself, you'll understand what the affection of a beloved person could mean to you. In the next chapter I have included a dairy (logbook) of my trauma-meditations. In that log you'll be able to read about examples of both my trauma-meditations and my trauma-paradise. But first I'm going to explain to you what exactly the logbook means.

Step 5. Writing therapy

Every flying instructor has a logbook in which he registers all flights. It's important that you yourself also keep a logbook. In this logbook you'll have to take notes of your experiences during your trauma-meditations. Keeping a logbook has three objectives.

Firstly: After six months I'm going to read my logbook again. The reason why I'm going to do this, is to check the influence of the contents (healed traumas) on my emotions. This is a post-control (after-check) in the form of an emotional check-up. If I should meet traumatic experiences, which still might evoke the remainders of nasty emotions inside me, I'm going to treat them once more during the next trauma-meditation.

Secondly: By writing down your trauma-meditations, you're creating an additional distance from your trauma-experience. Why? What's the difference between your trauma-experience, which is reproduced in your memory and your trauma-experience which has been written down? It's the same difference as which exists between a webpage which is shown on your computer screen and a webpage which you have printed on a sheet of paper. The webpage suddenly becomes tangible. You can tear this webpage into little pieces of paper, you can burn it, you can make a book out of it or you can fold it in the shape of an airplane. You can make twenty airplanes, go to a high place, for instance the roof of a high building or a place like the Statue of Liberty in New York or the Eifel tower in Paris and let the wind take them along. This is a way to express a ritual farewell to your traumas. I choose to write a book about my way of dealing with my traumas.

Thirdly. When writing down your trauma-experience, you're reliving your nasty (bad) traumas all over again. Sometimes I feel that my trauma-meditation is exposing a hidden emotion, which is emerging while I'm writing. This way a tremendous feeling of guilt emerged after my trauma-meditation about my deceased dog. Writing it out of your system (mind), in other words writing about your emotions, could have a therapeutical and healing effect. It could help just like telling a story. Writing is effective and sometimes even better than talking. Writing it out of your mind is a key issue in a so-called writing therapy which is used by psychologists.

Logbook of my trauma-meditations

In one trauma-meditation I treat several traumas. After having treated the first trauma, I'm going to set the same mousetrap for the next trauma immediately. I'm going to repeat this procedure until the target-feeling (almost) disappears or drops beneath a level of 10 percent.

August 22

I'm a committee member of a foundation. A complaint is being submitted.

"I'm going to submit a complaint with a television program concerning the way of doing business by your organization. Dirty swindlers (crooks)". Henk

Rather rude language. I don't understand a single word of what that man means. Who's this man called "Henk"? I don't know him. He hasn't added his surname. What way of doing business is he referring to? Commonly it's the very first time that a complaint is being submitted at our department and moreover in this disrespectful manner. I feel all kinds of emotions stirring inside me: fear, agitation, a stuck feeling in my throat. My "I-ego" is arousing and pulls back in defense. I feel being attacked and being personally handled disrespectfully. I would really like to send him a very angry email in return, putting him straight into the place he deserves. But I shall not do this. I don't want to start writing out of my bad emotions. Whatever is going to happen, I want to remain calm and customer friendly. I'm going to meditate.

Target-feeling

I concentrate on that feeling in my throat and I let my mind do its job.

Image

The first trauma from my youth emerges. I'm a child of about eight years old and I'm playing outside. A big man said to me in a threatening way that I should bring "the thing" to him tomorrow. I'm getting very afraid. (The day before my mother had frightened me by warning me by all means not to lose the key of our house, because in that case we could be robbed!). I immediately conclude that "that thing" had to be the key of our house. I run away, go home and I lock myself up from the inside. Overwhelmed by fear and stress I fall into a deep sleep. It's late in the afternoon. I awake caused by noises in the kitchen. A man is creeping inside through the kitchen window. A wave of bestial fear is washing over my body. I scream out of the depth of my belly and I try to push him back outside. I see that underneath our window (we lived on the ground floor) many of our neighbors, my mother and other spectators are standing and laughing. I'm in a state of shock caused by being scared stiff, my nerves are tremendously overstrained and I'm being laughed at by the whole neighbourhood and on top of that also by kids of my own age.

It's time for the flying instructor to intervene.

I visualize a glass wall between that man and myself. I embrace the child in the warm blanket of my love. His body is starting to relax from the shock and slowly he's falling deeply asleep in my arms. I take him with me to my trauma-paradise. We're gliding through a tunnel and we're tumbling directly into the water of the lake, like people do in an amusement waterpark. All my trauma-children are playing there in a continuous state of love and joy. Unfortunately it does not help. He's not feeling happy there right now and he isn't joining the other children playing in the lake. I'm taking him in my heart and keep embracing him with all the love I've got. It helps. Slowly he begins to relax in my embrace. When I recall the image of the kitchen with the man in the window, I see a thick glass wall between him and my surronnding area. It's feeling safe. I don't feel fear any more.

PS: What has happened? Who was that man who asked me to bring "the thing? I have never told my mother about that man because I was so terrifying afraid of him. Years later I found out that that man was retarded.

Who was the man who crawled through the window? My mother couldn't enter the house because I had locked myself up from the inside. She did ring at the door, but I didn't hear her because I slept like a log. That's why she called in a neighbor who tried to get into the kitchen though the small window in order to open the door from the inside.

Back to the target-feeling.

I resume meditating. The emotions in my throat, on which I'm concentrating, are lessening. I resume intensifying my concentration on these emotions.

Image

I'm confronted with the second trauma. Little Filipp (4 or 5 years old) is left behind on a street in an unknown part of the city. He's terribly afraid and he's crying. He doesn't know where his grandmother is and if she will ever come back. His survival fear and his fear of an unknown future are bigger than he himself. There is nobody around him. I embrace little Filipp with the warm blanket and I take him in my arms. I give him my love. Slowly he's starting to unwind and to relax until finally he's falling into a deep sleep. I try to let him glide downwards into my trauma-child-paradise. He's feeling unhappy there, because he has not yet been able to come to terms with his sorrow. I'm taking him back into my heart and I'm embracing him with my love. Finally it helps.

Back to the target-feeling

I return to concentrate myself on that feeling.

Image

A third trauma is coming. Little Filipp (4 years old) is in the day-care centre. Something happens, not something awful but something minor and unimportant, but all children are surrounding little Filipp and start to laugh at him. What I'm feeling comes close to the emotions the earlier mentioned complaint by email evoked in me. I'm trying to give my love to little Filipp and to send him to my trauma-paradise. Both actions do not help. They fail to change the experience little Filipp is under-going. The feeling is not going to disappear. If I'm not going to be able to change his inner experience, I might be able to change the situation. The solution appears by itself. Little Filipp gets hold of a garden hose and starts spraying everybody with water. Children are screaming and try to run away. Most of them are soaking wet, so that you can see their underwear through their dresses and T-shirts. Little Filipp is now feeling a lot better. His negative feelings are disappearing like snow in the sun. Suddenly I see the tender loving eyes of a little girl from my group. She's all wet, but she keeps standing before little Filipp and looks at him with her eyes full of love. My mother told me that this little girl always took care of me and even dressed me when I was a little child. She and I are looking into each other's eyes. I sense the inner rest slowly filling my body and soul. It's working.

My target-feeling is almost gone. There still might be a little remainder. When I'm rereading the complaint, I'm not bothered by restlessness, fear and negative feelings any more. I keep calm without doing anything. There's still just a little bit of that nasty feeling in my throat. I'm going to "treat" that in my next meditation. I now understand that I should be grateful to that gentleman uttering his complaint. He has brought forgotten traumas, which were locked up inside me, to the surface.

August 22

After my trauma-meditation about the complaint, I have not been bothered about fear and restlessness anymore! Yet I notice that unconsciously I'm preoccupied with the complaint. It's a sense of waiting for what's going to happen. I'm waiting for an answer from that mister Henk, who has been writing down the complaint. In all quietness I wrote an email to Mr. Henk asking him friendly for an explanation of his complaint. Waiting for the unknown, for the things to come, keeps me very much preoccupied, noticeable through a vague feeling and a light tension. I'm still sensing a slight remnant (remainder) of the stuck "shit" feeling in my throat. It's time to meditate again.

Target-feeling

I'm concentrating myself on the feeling in my throat. I allow my mind to relax and I'm awaiting the things to come.

Image

An image is appearing. At school I have been pestered and laughed at. A boy, being two years older than I am but also being a lot smaller, has kicked me in the ass several times. It was alternated by spitting at me. The rest of his friends were standing around, enjoying "the show". Every spitting or kick in the ass is being accompanied by laughing and comments. I'm at full strain while awaiting the next of his provocations. What is he going to do now? Spitting, kicking or something else? I'm feeling that I cannot do anything to protect myself. It's not the first time that I'm being bullied by them. He and his friends are always having the situation in their power. Waiting for their next kick or their spitting while being powerless and sad, puts me to enormous stress (so that's where stress is coming from!).

Because I was quite tall for my age, I was a favourite target for the elder boys. Especially one of them always used to like bullying me a lot. Because he was much smaller than the other boys of his age, he continuously had to look for self-affirmation by disparaging and pestering me. It wasn't the first time that he "treated "me that way.

It was time to intervene.

I'm trying to help myself. Filipp is going through his adolescence. I notice that he's behaving differently when I'm taking him in my warm blanket and I'm trying to give him love. The reason is that he dislikes it. He doesn't want to be comforted like a child. My trauma-paradise doesn't work either! What to do now? I try to ask him what he needs. He wants to be protected from the rest to be able to first go fighting with the one who's bullying him the most of all. I separate him from the rest by placing a glass wall between them and I let him fight it out with that boy. It's going well, Filipp is the one who's handing out the smacks. After every hit Filipp is feeling better until the boy is going down by a final hit. Filipp is the winner, but his nasty emotions are coming back. It does not work. What to do now? I try to make a fool of the beaten boy. Filipp gets a rope in his hands. His opponent is now tied up by his legs, he's hanging upside down right on top of a lavatory hole full of shit. Filipp is letting him drop into the hole all the time. His head is being covered by the brown coloured shit rests. Filipp bursts out laughing at first, but soon he's going to feel sorry for the boy and he sets him loose and he's letting him go. Filipp feels that he would rather have been embracing this boy with loving care instead.

So this doesn't work either. What to do now? The feeling is still there. Suddenly I see Filipp bending before the feet of the boy like a monk is used to do in front of Buddha. Now that boy seems to be the winner. The forehead of Filipp is touching the floor. The boy is being confused by that move. He's mumbling something. I see different feelings reflecting in his eyes, which are constantly relieving each other. He now doesn't know how to behave anymore. He feels a lot of shame and uneasiness and he don't want to lose his image in front of his friends. A miracle has happened! It's working! The bad feeling I had before this trauma is gone.

Back to the target-feeling.

I return my attention to my target-feeling. It has become smaller but the nasty feeling is still there. I concentrate myself on that feeling.

Image

An image is appearing. I'm at home. It's about six o'clock. I know that soon my mother will be coming home from her work. I'm very tense what's going to happen this time. Often my mother used to come home from her work in an "agitated" mood. Every time a wave of verbal violence, swearing, intimidating and disparaging came along. My body is in a state of continuous tension. My nerves are stretched like the strings of a guitar. I see myself in this state waiting for her in our house. I want to help little Filipp. My loving blanket does not help. I notice dat the loving care of the blanket as well as the trauma-paradise are not helping any more when I got older. I hear my mother entering the house. I solidly close the room in which little Filipp is sitting anxiously. Once more I visualize a thick glass wall, to protect him from his mother. He's safe now. I'm going to sit facing him and we look into each other's eyes. I don't know how to be able to help him right now. He says to me:" Do not worry. It's okay. It's my task to stay here". He has the eyes of an old wise man. Caused by his words I'm feeling a wave of inner rest coming over us. The target-feeling is gone.

Post-control of my target-feeling.

The intensity of my target-feeling has been lowered from 10 to 1. In other words; It has been reduced with 90%. I know from experience that the remaining 10 percent will automatically go away by itself.

PS: I never received an answer to my email from that mister Henk. In my thoughts I nevertheless thank mister Henk for his earlier email containing his complaint.

August 27

I'm feeling a bit sick. My stomach is bothering me, I have feelings of nausea, I'm very tired and I'm feeling weak. Especially feelings of nausea, which are present in the background of my system. I can feel it. I'm going to meditate.

Target-feeling

I'm going to concentrate on that feeling of nausea.

Image

I see myself (being 8 till 9 years old) in a hospital. I'm being hospitalized and examined. I'm feeling very ill. I'm also very sick in my stomach, I'm tired, I'm feeling light in my head and I'm so weak that I'm hardly able to stand upright. However the doctor wants me to remain standing upright for the benefit of her examination. All of a sudden everything turns black and I faint. The image of this incident is disappearing.

Back to the target-feeling.

I resume concentrating on the target-feeling.

Image

I'm seeing a sad little Filipp, who's crying. I take him into my arms and I give him my love (loving care). He's feeling better now. I have been holding him close to my body with all my love.

Back to the target-feeling.

I resume concentrating on the target-feeling.

Image

I'm seeing Filipp, his age being twelve to thirteen years old. His dog has died. Filipp loved him a lot. He's not being able to cry. He's sitting on the couch, holding back his grief. I'm going to sit on the couch next to Filipp. I take him in my arms and I kiss him on his forehead. I'm doing all this with the love of a mother. He's accepting this and he surrenders to this loving kind of care. Slowly he's beginning to cry. It's getting increasingly intense. He's crying his heart out now. I feel the lump of grief in his throat slowly melting away. He's still in my arms. Eventually Filipp has stopped crying. He's feeling relieved. I take him into my heart. Afterwards I send him to my trauma-paradise. I was surprised to see that he's feeling happy there.

Back to the target-feeling.

I resume concentrating on my target-feeling.

Image

I see little Filipp swimming in the sea. He's got water in his mouth and in his bronchial tubes. He's couching out the seawater. It isn't a nice sight. I try to embrace him, to give him love, to comfort him, to be a "mother" for him. He's accepting it, he rapidly gains his breath. Moreover he doesn't want to go to my trauma-paradise. He prefers to return to the seaside to play and to swim. He's cheerful again.

Post control of my target-feeling.

It's almost gone. The target-feeling is now below 10 percent.

August 31

Next to my house is a primary school. Every afternoon mothers with their bicycles and cars are coming there to pick up their children. I notice that those mothers, who are so careful about their children, are giving me a feeling of irritation and suppressed anger. I have decided to do something about it.

Meditation. I'm evoking an image of the school and the waiting mothers. The feeling of irritation/anger is slowly entering my body. I now clearly sense the spot in my body where this feeling is concentrated. It looks like a heave block which is situated in the solar plexus, a place which is located a few centimeters above the navel.

Target-feeling

I concentrate on that block in my solar plexus.

Image

Suddenly I feel a slap in my face. Somebody has hit me hard with a fist. It hurts co much, that I feel the effect of it in my skull. Apart from that I'm not getting any image at all.

Back to the target-feeling.

I resume concentrating on the target-feeling.

Image

I'm seeing myself. Little Filipp is about three years old and he's playing in a sandbox together with other children. He's very angry and he doesn't know what to do. There are no adults nearby. Little Filipp is throwing sand at another child (wrongdoer). I'm taking little Filipp in my arms, give him love and I try to take him to the trauma-paradise. He doesn't want to, he's feeling better now and he wants to stay in the sandbox. So I allow him to keep on playing in the sandbox.

Back to the target-feeling

I resume concentrating on the target-feeling.

Little Filipp 1 year old with his mother in 1978

Little Filipp 1 year old with his mother in 1978

Little Filipp 1 year old with his grandmother in 1978

Little Filipp 3 years old with his mother in 1980

Little Filipp 3 years old with his mother in 1980

Little Filipp 3 years old with his mother in 1980

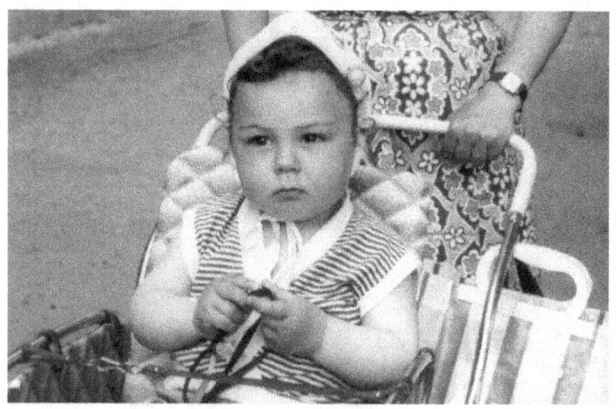

Little Filipp 1 year old in 1978

Little Filipp 3 years old in 1980

Little Filipp 7 years old in 1984

Filipp 11 years old in 1988

Image

I'm seeing Little Filipp (three years old) crying in the arms of his grandmother. He suffers a lot of pain as he has been falling on his head. I embrace my grandmother and little Filipp, give them love an take them to the trauma-paradise. They are being well received. There are living several little Filipp's who have found their inner peace of mind and happiness in the trauma-paradise. Everybody is running to our grandmother and they want a hug from her. Little Filipp is feeling fine now, he's forgetting his pain and he starts to play with "the other little Filipp's".

Back to the target-feeling.

I resume concentrating on the target-feeling.

Image

I'm seeing little Filipp. Children are spitting on him. They are spitting that much, that he can't do anything about it. There are no adults nearby. Little Filipp is feeling alone, sad and powerless. I pull a glass dome over and around little Filipp take him in my arms and give him my love.

After that I'm calling for the assistance of a big spitting machine. The machine is spitting at all children till they are covered with a thick layer of spit all over. It looks like spitclots of an elephant. Little Filipp can't help laughing while seeing this. I let him glide into my trauma-paradise, where he meets his grandmother and other little Filipp's. He's feeling happy there.

Back to the target-feeling.

I resume concentrating on the target-feeling.

Image

I'm seeing little Filipp on a party at school, where a lot of children are present. The parents of the children are also present and they are very proud of their children. His mother isn't there… Little Filipp is feeling abandoned. Maybe his mother is coming later on? I take little Filipp into my arms, I give him my love and I send him to my trauma-paradise. It takes effect.

Back to the target-feeling.

I notice that my target-feeling is beginning to disappear. Now it's more a smeared out feeling between my throat and my solar plexus. I'm concentrating on that.

Image

Another slap in my face. The same fist. Pain in my chest. I take little Filipp in my hands an give him my loving care. I put a stone wall between us and the fist. The fist is going right through the wall. I install a thicker wall, this time made of concrete. I hear the fist hammering against the wall and it's hurting itself quite a lot. I haven't the faintest idea what's the meaning of that and to which memory it's related. I take little Filipp to my trauma-paradise. Little Filipp is now feeling safe and protected.

Post-control of my target-feeling.

I resume concentrating on the target-feeling. It's almost gone. There still is a tiny-weeny rest in my throat. I feel different now, I feel space which came into existence on the spot where the block used to be. I'm feeling lighter now. I feel my breath coming deeper into my belly.

September 2

This morning I went to a meeting. We talked about cutbacks (to be) realized by the government. By doing so the most vulnerable people are going to get into a lot of misery. After the meeting I felt a lump in my throat. I couldn't get rid of it. In the bus I started to practice the trauma-meditation.

Target-feeling

I'm concentrating on the lump in my throat and I keep waiting.

Image

I'm seeing an image. I see a little Filipp (younger than

three years old) being completely upset and crying. His body is trembling all over. His mother is with him. She's furious. She's yelling at him. There is a lot of verbal violence. Little Filipp puts his little hands in the air to protect himself against his mother. She grabs him and she roiughly shakes him up. It's time for me to interfere. I wrap little Filipp in my blanket, embrace him and give him my loving care. It's no use at the moment. The threat caused by my mother is still there. He's afraid that she is going to beat him to death. I'm visualizing bars and I put my mother behind them. I see her putting her hands in anger through the bars. She's trying to grab little Filipp. He is terrified. I'm tying my mother up in a long white straitjacket, like they use to do with psychiatric patients who are totally upset. The sleeves are being tied up on her breast. My mother keeps resisting. The image of my mother behind bars tied up in that straitjacket does good. Little Filipp is beginning to relax with me. He's slowly recovering and I take him into my heart. I let little Filipp glide into my trauma-paradise. After his arrival he's being taken care of by his grandmother. Little Filipp is very glad to see her. He grabs her dress with his little hands and he doesn't want to let go of her. Gradually he gets accustomed to the surrounding area and his attention is being drawn by other playing little Filipp's and by little fish in the water. Finally little Filipp's hand releases the dress of his grandmother to go join the other little Filipp's playing in the water. He's going to be all right. I'm convinced of that.

Back to the target-feeling.

I resume concentrating on the target-feeling.

Image.

I'm seeing little Filipp (younger than 4 years old). He's playing in a river and he unfortunately ended up in deep water. He's underwater now. The water comes into his throat and he's beginning to gulp it down. All of a sudden he's being dragged out of the water. He has to cough very heavily. There's water coming out of his nose and mouth.

I'm taking little Filipp in my arms and I put him in my lap. He's almost choking and he has to cough quite a lot. I try to assist him, giving him my loving care. Little Filipp can't stop couching yet. But at last slowly but surely his breathing starts getting back to normal and only the taste of the river water still remains in his mouth and throat for a while. I give him a juice and he eagerly drinks it. I also give him a banana. He's fond of that too. Gradually his attention returns to the shallow water, where little newborn fish are swimming around. He's still sitting on my lap. Little Filipp is feeling better. I take him to my trauma-paradise.

Back to the target-feeling.

I resume concentrating on the target-feeling. I feel that I'm going to get very sick in the stomach.

Image.

I'm going through my puberty. It comes out of my stomach. I drank a glass filled with kerosene. Explanation of the situation: My mother forced me to. My tonsils were troubling me a lot. They were frequently inflamed as a result of which I regularly caught a flu or a cold. My mother never felt like looking after me when I became ill. When I caught a cold it was always my own fault and then she got angry and grouchy. As my mother had heard somewhere that kerosene should cure these illnesses, she was totally convinced that this was true. I was forced by her to drink a glass of kerosene. I didn't want to. After verbally "handling" me for days (by means of belittling, blackmailing, pestering, saying that I'm not a real man), finally I gave up and I drank a glass of kerosene. In fact at that time I couldn't care less any more whether I might die of the consequences or not. I felt apathetic and depressed. What happened next, has been wiped out of my memory. I'm (now) feeling very nauseating but it won't come out of my stomach. I've got a terrible taste of kerosene in my throat and in my mouth. I feel the cold sweat appearing on my forehead, under my nose and on my back. I'm feeling terribly miserable and weak. It's all got stuck up. I'm not being able to throw up at all.

NB I'm still in the bus on my way home. I'm feeling so miserable, that I'll have to stop meditating. As soon as I got home I'll try to resume meditating.

Finally I'm at home. I'm going to resume meditating. I'm concentrating myself on the nausea. Within two minutes I jump (out of the meditation chair) and rush to the toilet. I have to puke very badly. I'm hanging above the toilet bowl. My stomach is shrinking, I'm having terrible vomit convulsions, but still nothing is coming out of my stomach. I feel terrible. Like this I keep on trying to vomit for a quarter of an hour, cling-ing to the toilet bowl. But still nothing is coming out. I feel my stomach turning inside out. I feel the gut walls contracting constantly. I vomit, I vomit and I keep on vomiting. My eyes are filled with tears because of the vomiting. I have to take deep breaths. The urge to vom-it is diminishing a bit. Again I'm focusing on my stom-ach and again I have to vomit awfully. I keep on inhal-ing deeply followed by another throw up, until the urge to vomit is gradually going to slow down. After half an hour it's becoming quiet, I'm still sitting on the floor clinging to my toilet bowl. I'm looking into the bowl and I'm looking at my own reflection in the water. I'm exhausted and I'm soaking wet caused by my own sweat. I'm lying down for a few moments, but almost immediately I'm getting up again. I want to continue my meditation. I persist to get through with it.

I'm concentrating again on my nausea. Again I'm feeling Filipp from the meditation in the bus. After a lot of suffering at last he was being able to throw up. I'm still tasting the heartburn in his mouth and throat. It's also the taste of my own vomit. I'm still experiencing the poisonous taste of the kerosene, but it's out of my body now. I'm very exhausted, I'm going to lie down and almost immediately I'm falling into a deep sleep. After two hours I wake up. I'm still feeling very tired, it feels as if my stomach went through this ordeal only two hours ago. I feel my stomach from the inside. It's empty now. I'm only still feeling the nasty aftertaste of the kerosene in my mouth, but I'm not sick in the stomach anymore. I made it! I coped with it!

September 3 and 4

I'm not feeling well. I suffer from my stomach, I'm a bit nauseous, I have no energy at all and I'm very tired. During the daytime I'm sleeping a lot. I sense that my stomach is being under pressure.

September 5

I'm feeling a little bit better, but still not really well. My mind is 'overloaded'. I'm dreaming quite a lot, as a result of which I'm sleeping restless and I'm not reposing well. In my meditations I can't endure trauma's. I merely push them away. At the moment I haven't got the energy to handle them.

September 6

I understand that I'll have to get my trauma's out of my subconsciousness piece by piece. These pieces are not allowed to be bigger than my inner space, being the available space in my mind, at that particular moment. I feel that right now my mind is overloaded. Resting and meditating in a relaxed way are the only things that I'm capable to do at this moment. No trauma-meditations for the time being.

September 7

I'm feeling a lump of nasty emotions stuck in my solar plexus. I decide to treat this situation during a trauma-meditation.

Target-feeling

I'm concentrating on the lump in my solar plexus. I feel that my stomach is very tense.

Image

I'm seeing myself lying in a hospital. Philippe is 23 years old and he's suffering from a heavy burn-out. Philippe is having a relationship. His mother is fiercely against it. She's expressing her disapproval by means of blackmail, manipulations and verbal violence. She's constantly manipulating the feelings of Philippe. His nerves, stomach and heart cannot endure this any longer and he ends up in a hospital. Philippe has just been hospitalized. At first he's lying on the intensive care because of his heart problems. They are taking blood from him. He's feeling weak, nauseating and so miserable, that he isn't feeling his stomach anymore. It's becoming very light in his head. Philippe is on the edge of his consciousness. Al of a sudden I can't see a thing anymore. Everything is black. Philippe has fainted. He smells the terrible stench of some kind of medicine which they are holding under his nostrils to bring him back to his consciousness. Slowly the image is coming back. He's still feeling terribly miserable.

I'm taking Philippe into my arms. He's hardly aware of himself. I embrace him and I let him glide into my trauma-paradise. There he's lovingly being taken care of by his grandmother. She lays him on a bed at the side of the lake and she's looking after him with all of her loving care. She gives him a lot of tasty food, attention and love. Gradually he's going to feel better.

Back to the target-feeling.

I resume concentrating on my solar plexus.

Image

I'm seeing Philippe (20 years old) in another hospital. He's lying on the floor unconsciously. He opens his eyes and he's looking at the trap of the drain pipe. He was on his way to the toilet and suddenly he lost his consciousness. He's lying under neath a sink in his room. Because he's all alone there, nobody knows how long he has been lying on that spot. He creeps on the floor towards the door and he calls out for help.

I was hospitalized with a sturdy inflammation of my tonsils. My tonsils had become so big, that I could hardly eat something. As swallowing did hurt very much, the only food I was able to get through my throat was liquid nutrition. I was alone in my room. A few moments ago a nurse came in to give me a very painful injection. I did my utmost not to scream. She has left the room. Suddenly I got unwell. I started feeling very light in my head. I felt all energy flowing out of my body. Suddenly I became very weak and I felt miserable. My stomach turned and I had to throw up. I went to the toilet and there I lost my conscience.

I embraced Philippe and I took him to the trauma-paradise right away. He's lying in a bed next to the bed of the other sick Philippe. My grandmother takes care of them with her loving care.

Back to the target-feeling.

I'm concentrating on the lump in my solar plexus.

Image

I'm seeing myself in the admission room of a hospital. Little Filipp is about eight years old. The doctor asks him to go standing upright to be able to listen to his lungs. He's feeling very weak, nauseating and light in his head. All of a sudden his sight is turning black. He's losing his conscience and he drops to the floor.

NB I had been hospitalized with Hepatitis B after having eaten almost nothing during a couple of weeks. I stayed at the hospital for a month.

I also sent this little Filipp to the trauma-paradise. He's lying in a bed next to the bed of the other little Filipp. My grandmother took care of them with all her love.

Post control of my target-feeling.

It's almost gone. The target-feeling is now below 10 percent.

Afternoon. After the meditation. Occasionally I'm getting a rising happy feeling. This only lasts for a few moments, but it's feeling very nice.

September 9

During the last few days a whole range of memories (many of them from the first years of my life) came along. A few of them are giving me a good feeling, while the other ones are neutral, giving me neither good or bad feelings.

I think that my last trauma-meditations has caused a shift in my memory. A part of the frozen recollections has been melted out of the iceberg.

October 3

Of late I'm often short of breath. I have the tightness of my chest being examined in a hospital. After having undergone an MRI scan, an X-ray of my lungs and other tests, my doctor came to the conclusion that physically there was nothing wrong with me and that the tightness of my chest was caused by psychological factors. During one of my latest meditations I suddenly became extremely short of breath. I was choking so badly, that I almost fainted. I didn't get a clue or another indication where it could have come from. The only thing I know is, that the tightness of my chest is especially occurring on moments of intense fatigue. I wonder what the exact reason of this complaint might be.

Target-feeling

I'm concentrating on the feeling of tightness of my chest.

Image

A recollection is entering my consciousness. Filipp can't breath. He's choking on cement dust. (When I was thirteen years old, I worked at a concrete- & construction-factory during the school holidays. The factory was specialized in building projects and it produced concrete and various building materials. I was employed in the production of building materials and concrete, during which I was continuously exposed to the cement dust. I was working in a shed where unpacked cement was stored. In the shed about four railway carriages filled with cement could be kept. The cracks between the doors and the frames, in the windows as well as in the other openings of the shed, were being covered with tape to prevent the cement from escaping to the outside and the humidity from entering the shed. All this had been done to preserve the cement. Regularly tank lorries carrying cement came to the shed. They disposed of a big hose which looked like the trunk of an elephant, through which the cement was being pumped inside the shed by means of a small round gap in the door. The ceiling, the walls and the doors inside the shed were covered with a gray layer of cement. The cement was everywhere. The cement dust was hanging in the air. Tons of cement were lying on the floor. It looked like a large gray skiing track. My job was to go inside the shed through a small side door, to fill up two large metal buckets with cement and to take those outside where I had to throw the cement from the buckets into a big cargo hold of an old lorry. As soon as the hold had been completely filled with cement, it was towed to a place where concrete was being produced. That way I have been inside the shed for hundreds of times a day to carry cement outside. During my work I inhaled a whole lot of this cement dust. While shoveling the cement into the buckets in the shed and discharging it into the cargo hold, all the time clouds of cement dust were set free in the air. Obviously I got these clouds of cement right into my face. At the end of my working days my eyelashes were gray and my face was covered with a layer of cement dust. You could write your name on my face with your finger if you wanted to. Every evening I was busy wiping my nose, which was filled up with cement dust. During my work I was deprived of a mouth mask or any other means of protection. This way I have been working fulltime for months in a row. Gradually I began to suffer from breathing problems and heavy coughing. On a certain moment I couldn't breathe anymore. I opened my mouth, I tried to inhale deeply but the air wouldn't go in. I almost choked so badly, that I often became panic stricken. I suffered a lot from fits of coughing. I coughed and coughed and coughed. Sometimes I wasn't able to stop coughing at all. It felt like something was stuck inside me and it wouldn't come out. A couple of months after my resignation I coughed a slimy ball out of my lungs. I squeezed the ball. It turned out that within the ball there was dry cement stucked together. During my work I increasingly began to suffer from extreme overtiredness as well as from dyspnoea. I felt totally exhausted and unwell but I kept on working. Real men are not complaining, as it was impressed on me.

During that period my overtiredness has started. I rapidly became short of breath and tired, even while performing a slight effort like climbing the stairs. At school I had to do physical exercises during the gymnastics lessons. I could hardly, or even not at all, perform them , because I was exhausted and very short of breath. That's why I got the lowest marks for the gymnastics lessons. My heart went beserc and I often got sick in the stomach caused by weariness. I also suffered from dizziness during that period. I often caught a cold and I regularly suffered from the flu. My resistance had almost disappeared.

I took Filipp with me to my trauma-paradise, where he is treated (looked after) by his grandmother.

October 23

I feel sorrow and a lump in my throat.

Target-feeling.

The lump in my throat. I'm concentrating on it.

Image

I'm seeing a little Filipp. Blood is being stinged out of his little finger. It's his very first time. He is between three and five years old. His mother is teasing him, calling him: "Crying cow". He is upset, awfully crying and screaming. She doesn't console him and she's not giving him any love at all. I take little Filipp by his hands and I embrace him. I give him all my love. He's slowly recovering, stops crying and is beginning to relax. I send him to our trauma-paradise, where he's lovingly being taken care of by his grandmother.

Back to the target-feeling.

Image.

I'm seeing little Filipp. He's still a very little child and he did it in his pants. His mother is furious, while little Filipp is crying awfully. She's yelling at him, she's laying him on his belly, grabs the legs of his trousers and in one movement she pulls his trousers off with a lot of violence. Little Filipp is being lifted up during the same rough movement and then he drops back on his belly. He's yelling and crying. This hasn't any benefit for him at all. His mother is ignoring him. I take him into my hands. He's completely upset. He's trembling all over. I embrace him and I give him my love. I send him to our trauma-paradise. He sees his grandmother and he's running towards her as fast as he can and falls into her arms. He's grabbing her so tight that he himself is hardly able to breath. He doesn't want to ever let her go away again. It isn't until this very moment that I sense how much he has missed her! The other little Filipp of "Crying cow" is sitting on the other half of her lap. They're both getting a piece of a watermelon and they don't intend to get off their grandmothers lap. Everything is going to be all right now. I can feel it.

Back to the target-feeling

Image

I'm seeing Filipp. He is sixteen years old. He's suffering from a lot of sorrow and mental pain. I try to embrace him but he pushes me away. He's too old now to be consoled that way. What to do now? I want to hear Filipp's story. I ask him to sit down. Slowly he starts telling about his way of sorrows.

F: She (the mother) doesn't understand me. I: How come? F: Because of her ignorance. She's never listening. She never wants to listen either. She's ignoring my needs. She tells me that I'll survive even without (fulfilling) my needs and that my feelings and problems are senseless. When I'm trying to talk to her about my feelings, she says: "DON'T YOU INVENT NON-

SENSE!". This hurts me a lot and it's giving me much grief. Quietly he starts crying.

I: Could it be helpful for you if I take you to your grandmother? F: I can't leave her (the mother) alone. I'm feeling immensely responsible for her. I: Does she feel the same for you too? P: No she doesn't, at least not concerning my emotions, my sorrow, pain or unhappiness. I think she's very afraid that I might make a mistake, which could damage other people. Then they're coming to recover the consequences of the damage from her. That's what she's very afraid of (i.e. that someone is going to hold her responsible for a mistake I made). I: Could it be helpful for you if I tell you that your mother is mentally ill? And that it might be better to leave her alone (at least for a while)? F: I'm afraid that she's going to die without me. Then I'll have nobody anymore. Then I'm left all alone in this world. I don't want this to happen. I love her. I embrace him and I ask him to come along to his grandmother. At last he reluctantly agrees to come along. We arrive in the trauma-paradise. He sees his grandmother, falls into her arms and bursts into tears. All of his heavy emotions are coming out of his system. She embraces him and she keeps holding his head on her shoulder. I ask her what we should do next. How can we help him? She's giving a sign, meaning: "Be quiet!" She says nothing. Filipp is crying in her arms. It lasts a long time. He's now feeling the love of his grandmother. He senses how every cell of his body is slowly beginning to relax. He's falling into a deep sleep. I notice that my breath is gradually becoming slower and deeper. I'm sleeping very deeply, but my consciousness is staying awake. Somewhere deep inside me I know it's the sleep of healing. I'm staying in this situation for forty minutes.

Post-control of my target-feeling.

The lump in my throat and my sorrow are both gone now.

October 28

I'm sad and I'm feeling lousy. I sense that because of this I'm getting negative thoughts as a result of which I'm beginning to feel depressed.

Target-feeling

My lousy feeling is situated somewhere in my throat.

Image

I'm seeing an image. A little Filipp who is crying. He's very upset. His mother doesn't want to console him. She's just ignoring him. Ignoring is her favourite technique out of her "education-toolbox". I embrace him with loving care and I send him to our trauma-paradise. He's being looked after with tender loving care by his grandmother.

Back to the target-feeling.

I'm seeing little Filipp (between 7 and 8 years old). He has fallen. Little Filipp has a wounded knee, but he isn't crying. I'm embracing him with tender loving care and I send him to our trauma-paradise. He's being well taken care of by his grandmother. She gives him love and consolation.

Back to the target-feeling.

Image

I'm seeing Philippe. He has been living in the Netherlands for ten years now. He's very sad and frustrated with his life. He's crying. He's feeling lonesome. Philippe has been harassed until he had to leave his own parental house in Russia, where he felt very unsafe. He's feeling like a fugitive, who fled from his mother and consequently from his motherland. He's doing his utmost to feel at home here in the Netherlands and he's trying to still make his life worthwhile. He's aiding other people through his foundation. This makes him feel as if his life hasn't been entirely useless by still providing him with something useful. He's doing his utmost. But all these efforts take a great deal of his energy and actually he should keep this energy for himself. He lost all connections with his inner feelings. He's living a stressed life caused by his constantly worrying (brooding) brains. He's exhausted and he's crying a lot.

I'm embracing him, I'm listening to him carefully and I'm having compassion with him. I'm giving him my love. I'm telling him that he doesn't have to face his misery all by himself. He's got ME!

I'm going to protect him, I will NOT allow ANY-BODY to cause him grief or injustice! I'm going to take care of him. I have taken Philippe into my heart. He's safe now.

Post control of my target-feeling.

My sorrow and my lousy feelings have been dropped below 10 percent.

November 4

I invented a new model. It's a pyramid. The pyramid is a hierarchical structuring of psychological factors which are playing an important role with regard to the ways people are making ends meet. I put the model on the internet with the intention to ask other people to give their opinion about it.

Regularly I receive reactions from people who are calling themselves experts on this subject. I immediately notice that they are not experts at all. They're by no means able to separate the content from the form. Their reactions are evoking in me a certain feeling of rebellion and anger. This is a perfect opportunity to do a trauma-meditation.

Target-feeling

My feeling of rebellion and anger. I'm concentrating on

the target-feeling.

Image

At once an image is appearing. Little Filipp is being beaten by his mother. She hurts him.

His mother is beating him while she's screaming and she does it with a lot of dedication (malicious devotion). Because of this the experience becomes all the more painful, especially in a psychological way of speaking.

I interfere. I put the mother behind a glass wall. She's furiously attacking the wall. She's acting extremely aggressive. Little Filipp is very afraid. I fasten her hands to the wall behind her with handcuffs. She's having a tantrum.

I take little Filipp in my arms. I'm giving him my loving care. I'm feeling it hasn't got the desired effect yet. He's trembling from panic and fear. His mind is somewhere far away driven by fear. After a while It's slowly returning into his body. He's beginning to relax and he's getting ready to accept my loving care. When he's finished coming to himself again, I send him to the trauma-paradise, where he's lovingly being taken care of by his grandmother. He's extremely happy to be in the safety of her presence.

Back to the target-feeling.

The target-feeling is diminishing.

Image

Again I'm seeing a group of youngsters harassing Filipp at school. Once more there's a boy belittling and intimidating Filipp. He's doing what he wants. That boy is two years older but a head's length shorter than Filipp. He's being supported by about eight of his friends who are enjoying the show and who are ready to come to the aid of their friend at any moment. He enjoys his power. Filipp knows two of this boys. They are his former neighbours from the time when he was still living on his previous address. One of them says that they are not going to stand up for Filipp, but that they are backing their "comrade", due to the fact that Filipp isn't living in their neighbourhood anymore and so he isn't one of them since he has moved. Trusted friends from his childhood suddenly turn out not to be friends anymore. They join the laughing at him and they're taking their new friend into protection. Filipp feels being betrayed. This gives him a lot of sorrow. The situation is hopeless. Filipp shall never be able to hold his own against the group. He's feeling ashamed and powerless, for there are a lot of "onlookers", among which also girls and boys from his own group.

I intervene. I'm pulling up a wall between them and Filipp. Bu this time Filipp only wants me to keep the group "at a distance". So I restrict myself to pulling up a glass wall around Filipp and the boy, so a sort of ring is being formed. This way the friends of the boy can't reach them. This time Filipp doesn't need any means such as boxing gloves. It appears that there's not going to be a fight. His adversary is getting very afraid. He even reacts anxious on every slight movement Filipp makes. His friends are laughing at him. Filipp feels the strength to defend himself returning, but the sorrow remains. It's a sorrow that has been caused by the fact that at first he had a lot of confidence in those two boys who had been his neighbours before he moved.

I don't know how to deal with that sorrow. I ask Filipp what he wants. "Let me look straight into their eyes". I let him do what he wants. Those two stop laughing at their friend, they feel ashamed, they try to hide their eyes. Filipp is looking into their eyes and he realizes that they never have been real friends to him. They are nothing but "hanger-ons". He feels his sorrow coming up again. "I have got no friends", Filipp says to me. I tell him that he surely has had friends. Together we go to his former neighbourhood. Filipp is looking for his real friends. He realizes that many of them are not real friends. A real friend should have protected him. And indeed there was such a person, who always protected Filipp against others! His name is Dima (Dimitry). Sometimes he even fought for Filipp, when he was still a very little boy. Dima also was a child of the same age as Filipp. Dima's father was an alcoholic. He was frequently drunk and then he used to beat up Dima's mother. Filipp now understands that Dima was his real friend. Now he's feeling sadness when he's thinking of Dima's family circumstances.

I don't know at once how to handle this. I'm aware that during my trauma-meditation a new layer of emotions has emerged. These are emotions behind other emotions. The iceberg is melting. I decide to take my sadness for Dima's family circumstances as my new target-feeling. I resume my trauma-meditation and I'm concentrating on this sadness. I'm seeing an image. Little Filipp is very little. For the first time in his life he's seeing a corpse. It's a well-known old woman next door, who has always been nice to little Filipp giving him sweets and cookies and so on. Little Filipp is afraid. He doesn't want to die, because he's afraid to be alone afterwards. I take him into my heart and I tell him that we will always stay together. Then I bring him to my trauma-paradise.

Back to the target-feeling.

The target-feeling has moved from 8 to 3. The anger is gone. It now has merely changed into a feeling of sorrow.

Image

I'm seeing little Filipp. He's lying in his bed and he can't sleep. On edge, strain in his head, worrying. He's looking at the carpet on the wall. He can't figure out his feelings and thoughts. I'm taking him in my arms, giving him my loving care. He's relaxing. I send him to my trauma-paradise.

Post-control of my target-feeling.

The target-feeling has dropped beneath 10 percent.

November 15

I'm restless lately. It's a feeling. I'm in a hurry. I can't afford to lose time anymore and I haven't the faintest idea where that feeling comes from. Could this perhaps has to do with my fear of failure? Could I be afraid to fail? But in that case I should have a purpose, an expectation or a wish to fulfill something in this life. If I don't have any of those, I couldn't possibly fail either. Or could this be an inner struggle with my traumatic youth and my mother? You see mother? I survived your "upbringing" and I made something out of my life all the same!

No, the feeling is located deeper. It's coming somewhere out of the middle of my breast. That's the place where the restlessness is concentrated. It's the love that wants to come to the outside. I still don't understand what it means exactly and how love can cause this restlessness. Is love in a hurry? Hurry for which purpose? I think I'm beginning to understand it now. I want to concentrate on the most important thing in my life and I want to achieve this by taking the shortest way towards it. The shortest way to the most important things in my life is going through my inner self. Far less important things like for instance internet, computers and reading about unimportant subjects are distracting me. My attention is continuously being distracted (most of the time by my own thoughts). I'm mixed up in a constant battle with my distractors. This makes me feel restless.

Mind

Am I serving my mind or is it the other way around? I'm constantly being carried away with the flow of my thoughts. My mind is merely a piece of equipment. It's a fork, a knife, a little scoop which I'm going to use when I really want to. Not the other way around! Unfortunately right now I'm not capable to control my restless mind. My mind is like a wild horse which doesn't allow anybody to ride on its back. No way! This wild horse would rather be dead than having to live under the custody of a master. The trick is not to try riding that wild horse, bur to set the animal free in her own nature and to let it be that way. I'm not my mind. My mind isn't my master. I don't want to carry out its mental fabrications. It has to be done the other way around! Just being a spectator of your own mind or looking at it from the outside is a good trick to prevent yourself from being the slave of your own mind. I do understand my mind all right. It's constantly being vexed and challenged. It's nature consists of continuously reflecting, classifying and trying to argue.

Every day sixty thousand thoughts are flying in all directions, consuming a lot of my energy. The mind is leading its own life, dragging me along. Who's in charge here? Not me. Can we live side by side without standing in each other's way?

Sometimes thinking is wonderful. When it's purposeful and it has a target that is being born out of love. It's flowing. It's in a flow. It is the flow. In such a case I'm excited and concentrated on my target for one hundred percent. Then my mind gets all the attention it needs from his owner. It's allowed to give my creativity a shape. It's glad like a dog that's getting a piece of chicken and the love of his owner at the very same time. It couldn't get enough of that.

In the meantime that animal runs towards all incentives. It creates its own world, mental towers which are called "logic" and sometimes it's looking at the inside of its owner. It's never looking at its own inside nature. Its attention is always directed to the outside. It's continuously looking for something to chew on. It's chewing on it until it sees something which seems to be still even more tasty. It then spits out the old chew and takes the fresh one. Only once in a while I'm appearing in its life. Tiresome....

November 28

I got my two dachshunds Morris and Florris when they were three and four years old. Their former owner got sick and she had to get rid of them. A year later I get a message from her telling me that she would like to come and visit my doggies. I immediately get a cocktail of emotions. I'm feeling afraid. It seems like somebody has got endless power over me on behalf of which he or she wants to take advantage of me.

Target-feeling

The cocktail is in my belly, right beneath the solar plexus. I'm concentrating on it.

Image

I'm seeing little Filipp, younger than five years old. He's walking on the street with his mother. Mamma is angry. Little Filipp is shaken and he's crying. Mamma is giving him a shaking and she pulls his hand frantically. (I'm feeling an enormous pain under my right armpit, the muscle strings are stretched out). Caused by the pain and her screaming little Filipp is walking down the street in a hysterical state of mind, loudly screaming and totally upset. He's screaming so loud, that people fifty metres away are turning around to see what's going on. Everybody is looking at us. Mamma quits the shaking and the cursing. She doesn't want their attention. Little Filipp has drawn too much attention on the street, as a result of which MAMMA is getting even more angry. Boiling with anger she drags little Filipp away from the street to be able to give her furiosity a "shape" somewhere else where she will not be disturbed. They're of the street now and little Filipp is again being beaten. I feel an enormous blow against my head. Little Filipp is in a terrible state of shock. It's horrible what

I'm feeling now. He's yelling MAMMA, MAMMA. He doesn't understand it at all anymore. It seems to him that somebody else is doing this to him. He's losing all contact with reality. He's screaming for help, protection and love from his MAMMA. He does love HIS Mamma. Where could she be now?

Little Filipp is losing every connection with reality as well as with himself. He's in severe state of shock and he's screaming like an animal out of the depth of his belly. It seems to me that he's behaving like a mental invalid. I interfere. I tie the hands of the mother to the wall. She keeps spitting out her hatred and anger like a ball of fire. She wants to finish little Filipp. I draw a glass wall all around her.

I take the body of little Filipp in my hands. There is no other way to describe him at this moment. It's a body. His consciousness is gone now. Love, or a banana or a tasty fruit juice don't help at this very moment. A heavy trauma has settled itself inside him. His body is in a state of shock. It's as tense as a guitar string. Besides, inside him there is a cocktail filled with immense mental pain, sadness and his screaming/begging for love towards his mother. The image of his furious mother behind the glass wall isn't going to calm him down. He's still afraid of her. I send for an ambulance. A couple of big sturdy ambulance male nurses take hold of her and they are giving her an injection containing a sedative. Her rage is diminishing and she's getting drowsy. The nurses take her with them. This is taking effect. Little Filipp is becoming calmer. Slowly he's getting out of his state of shock. He's feeling his fast beating little heart and his breath returning. I give him my loving care and I take him with me to our trauma-paradise. There he's being lovingly taken care of by his grandmother. He's very glad to see her. She's embracing and kissing him and she's giving him her loving care. He's starting to relax and eventually he's falling into a deep sleep. I'm also very tired and I'm hardly able to stay awake. I'm going to lay down on the cough and I'm too falling into a deep sleep. After two hours I wake up. The target-feeling is gone now. I'm feeling relieved.

December 2

I have got a restless feeling. This feeling prevents me from being sick in a quiet way. It also prevents me from resting, whereas of all times I'm needing it right now. (I'm tired, I've got a headache, my eyes are hurting etc.)

Target-feeling

I'm concentrating on that restless feeling.

Image

I'm seeing a little Filipp, being not more than five years old. He has just been heavily knocked on his head by his mother. Once again she wasn't in a good mood.

The physical pain is so heavy, that little Filipp starts to scream like an animal. My mother is getting even more angry. That kind of screaming is strictly forbidden.

Imagine that our neighbours are hearing little Filipp screaming in that manner! What would they think about her! Instead of comforting me, she's just increasing her mental aggression. DON'T YOU SCREAM!!!! She says this with such a terrifying voice, that little Filipp is afraid that she's really going to do something fatal to him. Moreover she's frantically pulling his arm towards her to let her words penetrate "in the right way". Little Filipp is getting so frightened, that he's doing his utmost not to feel that kind of pain in his head and particularly not to scream that loud. He's sensing so much hate, boiling anger and aggression in her whole attitude, that he wants to shrink from his outside into his inside. He's trembling and he starts howling like a wolf with short intervals one after the other. Besides little Filipp is trying to muffle his crying as much as possible as a result of which his crying sounds like the howling of a wolf. (It's difficult for me to describe the influence of all this on my body. I feel every millimetre on the surface of my skin awaiting the next blow. She spit out her words with so much hatred, anger and aggression, that I could sense them within me. Every word startled my body. My whole body had become one big nerve. I let the image take its course for a short while to be able to consider in the meantime what has to be done).

I interfere. My mother is being wrapped up in vacuum plastic like a chicken. You can see her in the rumpled plastic. She now looks like a packaged chicken in the supermarket. Carefully I take little Filipp by his hands.

Fortunately I'm able to get in touch with him. He's now lying in my arms, I'm giving him a lot of love. I feel that he's getting calmer. His emotions are gradually becoming more stable. His head is aching clearly now, which was not quite perceptible when his emotions were still running through his mind in the background. I ask him if he likes to go to his grandmother. He nods. I'm holding him carefully in my hands as we're going to our trauma-paradise. There he's being taken care of by his grandmother. She's taking him in her loving arms. Later on she takes him to his bed. He can't sleep, he's restless. Grandma is whispering something into his little ear. I see a smile appearing on his little face. He's feeling secure and he's slowly falling asleep.

Back to the target-feeling.

Image

Little Filipp, only ten years old. He's ill and has a high fever. He's lying in his bed. From the kitchen comes a lot of hard noises, caused by his mother frantically throwing around pans and other objects. She's madly shouting again because little Filipp is ill. Little Filipp's body is scared stiff by every word she's shouting and every pan she's throwing. It's about him and his illness. He's at full strain and very restless. He wants to get up and not to be ill anymore, so his mother is going to stop being angry at him. He's not allowing himself to be ill anymore. This should not be, or else his mama is going to get angry again.

I separate little Filipp from his mother and I take him to a safe place. I give him my love and I bring him to our trauma-paradise. He's feeling safe there and he's slowly coming to (recovering). His grandmother is going to give him a lot of loving care and she'll treat him well.

Back to the target-feeling.

Image

There is still another case of the same kind. I'm also treating this in the same way as I did before. When I'm done, I'm feeling a lot of quietness and warmth in my chest. I feel that I'm going to fall into a deep sleep. I'm going to lie down on the couch. I spend the rest of the afternoon sleeping.

December 24 Mindfulness meditation

A mindfulness meditation. During the meditation I saw the face of my mother. For the first time in my life I could feel my love for her without having to endure enormous mental pain. This is a very good sign with regard to the improvement of coming to terms with my traumas! I said to her that I love her very much, despite everything she had done to me. In this life she's never going to know what she had done to me and my mental health (my traumas). She's locked up in her own small world. She'll never be able to leave her present world, where she's suffering continuously. That's why I sent her my love.

January 7

A few weeks ago I was attacked, while walking with my own dogs, by a big dog belonging to my neighbours. The big dog was not leashed. Fortunately this incident had a happy ending. Neither of both my dogs were grabbed by the big one. Yesterday evening I saw that dog again. Again he wasn't leashed. I got frightened, I felt powerless. I'm not being able to give my little dogs the protection they need. I didn't feel safe. I couldn't fall asleep, I was lying awake and worrying until one o'clock. I felt that my body was filled up with stress. I rose and I wrote a letter to the neighbours:

Dear neighbours,

I'm your neighbour, the owners of the two dachshunds. A few weeks ago your dog attacked my dogs. I couldn't avoid the attack because I hadn't seen your dog coming. Your dog wasn't leashed and he attacked us from behind fully unexpected on my stairs. The attack caused an enormous shock for both me and my dogs. Since then one of my dogs is afraid of other big dogs.

This is not the first incident. The first time happened this summer, when your dog wasn't leashed on the lawn just around the corner of our building. Fortunately at that time nothing happened.

Only one bite of a big dog could cause the death of a small dog. In the past I had a little dog. She was attacked by a big dog, who grabbed her in the middle like a piece of toy between her big jaws. The attack lasted only a few seconds. My reaction as a human being was too slow to prevent this from happening. It was a horrible experience. The holes caused by the bites of the attacking dog were clearly visible in the belly and the side of my dog. One could see her internal organs from the outside. Our veterinary surgeon told me that fortunately her internal organs were very nearly missed, because otherwise my dog would surely have died.

I have noticed that your dog is taken out while not being leashed. Because of this I don't feel secure to take my two little dogs out for a walk with your big dog walking freely around. I therefor kindly request you to take your dog out while she's being leashed from now on. Anyway, this also happens to be our communal (municipal) duty as being dog owners.

I sincerely hope to be allowed to count on your understanding and your responsibility.

Yours faithfully,

Philippe

Right now I'm sensing a cocktail of feelings, fear, powerlessness, danger and restlessness. I'm going to meditate.

Target-feeling

I'm concentrating on this cocktail.

Image

Immediately I see my other dog called Bars, who died a long time ago. I'm feeling guilty and full of sorrow. Bars is a big dog. He's still young, only nine months old. My mother is fed up with him and she forces me to get rid of him. I love him. I can't take leave of Bars. I propose to let him stay in our former garage a few blocks away. She doesn't care as long as "that animal" is out of HER house. During the whole day he's locked up in the garage. Once a day I bring him food and I take him out for a walk. There are no animal homes in Russia (at least not in those days). Many dogs are suffering from famine during their street life and eventually are being shot by the municipal department of vermin extermination. One day I found him dead in the garage. Maybe he had been poisoned, as often happens when a barking dog is disturbing someone. I shall never know if it happened like this. Nevertheless I'm feeling terribly guilty because of his death. I now wonder if I could have been able to prevent it from happening. I'm suffering from a lot of sorrow about him. I'm seeing his dead body lying before me in the dark just like that. His body is frozen stiff. It's a terrible experience. I want to scream caused by sorrow and pain. I never tried to find another owner for him no matter how difficult this was during the poverty of that time. I'm feeling terribly guilty. I would gladly sacrifice ten years of my life if I could be able to change this particular. part of my life. I still love him. Writing this down I start crying again. Why for God's sake, was I, a child of merely thirteen years old, so attached to that animal and why couldn't I let him go and try to find another owner for him? I know his soul didn't die and that somewhere and some-time we will be together again. A fact is, that in my life nearly nobody (with the exception of my girlfriend Yvonne and my grandmother) has loved me. Still I think that my mother loves me too, with the exception that the utterance of her love has turned out to end up in a violent shape (maltreatment). The only way I could share my love was with animals. That's why a dog means a lot more to me than merely a companion ani-mal on four legs.

I interfere. I'm sitting in a dark garage before the dead body of my dog. I let a lot of white light coming into the garage. I'm going to sit in the garage end start medi-tating.

While typing this trauma-meditation something is hap-pening to me. Suddenly I quit typing. I burst into tears.

A lot of grief is coming up. After a quarter of an hour I resume typing.

I take Bars into my heart. He will forever keep on living in my heart. I'll always continue loving him. For me he'll be staying alive forever. He's my beloved soulmate. I take him with me to my trauma-paradise. He's alive again. My dear Bars. He's running into the water and he starts to play with all the little Filipp's. They're throwing a ball which he likes to chase. On their turn the little Filipp's are chasing him. It's a pleasant crowded mess of splattering, running, laughing and joy. My other doggie, who died a long time ago, is also there. The two dogs are chasing each other. They're completely overwhelmed with happiness and joy. I go to them. Everyone is running towards me. I feel a lot of love. It's like coming home. We are playing and laughing. I'm giving tasty chicken legs to my dogs. The little Filipp's are also being treated to delicious things. Granny is also with us. Everybody is eating rather hurried., for nobody wants to lose time. The time to go on playing! Everybody wants to start running again, to splatter with water, to throw balls, to play and to laugh. After the lunch numerous burps and farts are being produced and the enjoyable mess is starting all over again. They're all going to stay alive for my sake. This is the place to which I can always return, where everybody is happy and love each other.

January 17

A few weeks ago I applied for a sickness benefit. Today I had a consultation with an insurance physician about the medical examination. By chance today is (also) my mother's birthday.

Anticipating this examination consultation, I had a lot of stress during the last few days. I was feeling that tired and strained, that I wasn't able to meditate. After a week full of stress and worrying, I now notice that my happy feeling in my chest has disappeared. Again I'm feeling nothing at all. I'm locked up in my head again and I'm completely exhausted. Suddenly I realize that, despite this difficult time, mentally I didn't have broken down. I don't suffer from heavily overloaded emotions, which used to make me very anxious and depressed in the past. I realize that thanks to my trauma-meditations, I escaped from the prison of heavy emotions. I'm very glad about this.

January 31

I'm feeling jammed sorrow in my throat.

Target-feeling

I'm concentrating on the feeling in my throat.

Image

I'm seeing an image. Little Filipp, no more than five years old, is at home. All alone. He's very afraid and he's crying. I take him into my arms and give him my loving care. He's becoming quiet. I take him with me to our trauma-paradise.

Back to the target-feeling

Image

Little Filipp in on a holiday with his grandmother in the town where she's living. The town lies at the Caspian Sea. He's feeling safe, beloved and relaxed at his grandmother 's. He's happy being with her. Now he's totally upset, crying and stressing because he has to return to his mother. I interfere. I take him into my arms and give him my loving care. Then I take him with me to our trauma-paradise, where he can be happy with his grandmother for always. He's pressing his head deep into her belly, as a result of which he can't see anything anymore. He's smelling the reliable scent of his dear grandmother. She embraces him. He's feeling safe and happy with her.

Back to the target-feeling

Image

Little Filipp, not being more than three years old, is crying very badly. He has already been crying that long, that he hasn't any tears left. Nobody is consoling him. I take him into my arms, giving him my loving care. He's getting quiet. I take him with me to the trauma-paradise.

Back to the target-feeling

Image

Little Filipp, being no more than three years old, did it in his pants. He's strained all over and he's afraid to be beaten once more. I take him with me to his grandmother in the trauma-paradise, where his little arse is being washed clean with a lot of loving care. He's relaxed now. (Once my mother told me that I had been admitted in the day-care centre in a group with other children. Because I was bigger than the other kids of my age, they placed me in a group with older children. They were one or two years older than me and they were already capable to prevent doing it in their pants. Because I couldn't yet manage that, I still regularly did it in my pants, which seemed to be reason enough for the woman educator to beat the hell out of me. My mother told me that I hided myself behind her the moment I saw the educator coming in our direction and that I immediately started to cry intensely. My mother then spoke with the educator and explained the situation. She didn't know that I was a lot younger and she was quite surprised that I was situated in her group. Since that conversation she has never again hit little Filipp)

February 1

I'm bargaining with someone. That someone is very insecure. First he tells me that he wants to think about my proposal, then he rejects my proposal and then he suddenly agrees and almost at the same time he's hesitating again and wants to think about it one more time. It's annoying me very much! But what makes it worse is the fact that most of all its driving me furious! I would very much want to know the reason of this. For walking around with this feeling is very difficult to endure.

Target-feeling

The feeling of anger. I'm concentrating on that.

Image

Little Filipp is very much afraid and he's living on the verge of his nerves. His mother is raging mad and she shouts at him: YOU'RE IRRITATING YOUR MOTHER AGAIN! I'M GOING TO GIVE YOU SUCH A BWLOW ON YOUR HEAD, THAT IT'S GOIING TO FLY AWAY FROM YOUR BODY LIKE A BALL AND YOU'LL NEVER BE ABLE TO STAND UP AGAIN! EVEN IF I'LL HAVE TO GO TO PRISON FOR THAT REASON, I'LL NEVER REGRET IT FOR ONE SINGLE MOMENT! Little Filipp is terrified that his mother is going to beat him to death. He's also very sad. He doesn't understand it. I interfere. Like in many other meditations I heal this trauma in the same way.

Back to the target-feeling

Image

Little Filipp is being beaten by his mother. Again with a lot of verbal violence. Like in many other meditations I handle this in the same way.

Back to the target-feeling

Image

Little Filipp is alone and he's very afraid. He's standing before a forest and he's scared of entering. Like in many other meditations I'll take care of this in the same way

Back to the target-feeling

Image

I wondered why I was feeling angry. Now I'm sensing the answer to that question. In that insecure person I recognize my mother. It seems as if that person is a lookalike of my mother. Both of them are very occupied with their own EGO, while on the inside they're very afraid and insecure. I'm feeling the same tremendous showing of my mother, who was always beating and maltreating me. And when she herself felt threatened by someone, she began using me as a shield. Afterwards her anger often was being unleashed on me.

Back to the target-feeling

Image

Filipp, between thirteen and fifteen years old, is walking alongside a railroad track. A train is overtaking (passing) him. He's cold an he's feeling lonely. I embrace him with a big warm blanket and I take him with me to the trauma-paradise. He sees his Granny (she's sitting on a little bench), he runs towards her, he falls into her arms and he bursts out in tears. He says that he's feeling all alone in the world. There's nobody, absolutely nobody, who loves him and who's protecting him against others who are pestering (harassing) him. I embrace both him and my grandmother. He's slowly recovering, caused by our loving care. Afterwards we take him to a part of our trauma-paradise, especially intended for kids who are thirteen years and older, among which also girls are present!

Post-control

My anger has now been lowered beneath 10 percent. Out of my experience I know that this is normal. My trauma wounds need now some time to heal up. This will take some days or weeks. Eventually my anger is going to disappear completely by itself.

February 6

I have a relationship with Yvonne. Yvonne is sixteen years older than I am. She's a wonderful, sensible and beautiful person, with regard to her inner nature as well as to her outward appearance. I love her very much. Our relationship has been going on for some years now. I don't feel her love for me anymore. Nevertheless I'm sure that she (also) still loves me very much. Unfortunately I sense that Yvonne is blocking her feeling(s). Even during our most intimate moments I feel an invisible wall between us. Since a couple of weeks it's hard for me to see her. Inside me something is happening, which makes me sad. Every time I manage to push it away by using a "switch of thoughts". This is a kind of semi-conscious skill, which I developed in my youth to be able to survive during my childhood. It means that I remove my attention from a strong emotion, like for instance sorrow and that I subsequently direct my attention on something strongly positive, which causes alternative positive or neutral feelings. I manage to realize this through switching my thoughts. During the past weeks I have been practicing the very same skill with regard to my feelings for Yvonne (my problem to see her, the sorrow). Now I know that my "switch of thoughts" is just giving me a temporary release from my nasty emotions.

According to the founder of psycho-analysis, the well-known psychiatrist Sigmund Freud, during our sleep our suppressed emotions are getting an expression in the shape of a dream. Below follows an example of this (proven) theory out of my own life.

February 7

Last night I dreamed quite a lot. In my dream I had no place to spend the night. My girlfriend Yvonne allowed me to use a non-occupied hotel room, which had been booked by a friend of hers (called Diny) but which she's not going to use. I'm walking around in the hotel, but I cannot find a room booked by Diny. I phone Yvonne and I ask her to help me. Her indications don't lead to a solution. I'm feeling an invisible wall between us. I'm begging for her love but I can't manage to get through to her inner feelings. I awake in the middle of the night and I can't sleep anymore. I'm feeling sorrow caused by her rejection of my love for her.

Target-feeling

The feeling is in my throat. A lot of grief. I'm concentrating on that feeling.

Image

I see an image. Little Filipp, not being older than five years old, is very sad. He's crying. He's longing for the love of his mother but she neglects him. She's standing at the gas cooker, with her back turned to him and she's ignoring his begging. He's feeling a huge wall between them which he isn't able to break through.

I take him into my arms and I'm giving him as much love as possible. Then I take him with me to our trauma-paradise. He sees his grandmother, runs to her and bursts out into a big crying fit. He's feeling an intense mental pain and grief, which is caused by his love for his mother. Little Filipp "dives" with his nose into the belly of his grandmother. He wants to return to

144

the source where he came from. Slowly he's recovering in the hands of his grandmother.

Back to the target-feeling

Image

Little Filipp is seven years old and he's staying in a youth camp. A couple of weeks already have passed by. He badly misses his mother. Every day he's waiting for her to come and he's counting the days. She arrives. She stays for a few hours and then she leaves. Little Filipp bursts out into an enormous crying fit. He has been missing her for such a long time and then she leaves after such a short time! I pass through this trauma in exactly the same manner.

Back to the target-feeling

Image

The same camp. His mother was going to come and visit him today. He hasn't seen his mother for a couple of weeks now. In all little Filipp is staying for two to three months a year in that same summer camp, where he isn't feeling happy at all. Already a week before her arrival little Filipp has been counting both the days and the hours. Immediately after having breakfast little Filipp runs to the gate of the camp and he sits on the ground outside the camp to wait for his mama to come. He keeps sitting on the ground and watching the road in the direction from where his mother is supposed to come. Little Filipp is waiting for his mama. It's after ten o'clock. She still hasn't arrived. He's counting the minutes. It's getting eleven o'clock, twelve o'clock. She's still not coming. It's about one o'clock. Little Filipp has got to go to the canteen to have lunch, otherwise he's going to stay without food during the rest of the day. He doesn't want to leave his waiting spot, because he's afraid that he might miss his mama.

I take him into my arms and I give him a lot of love. Next we go to his dear grandma, where he's slowly recovering.

Back to the target-feeling

Image

I'm seeing Yvon. There's a thick glass wall between us. Little Filipp is holding his little hands against the wall, as if he's trying to touch her. He wants to embrace her. Yvon is standing on the other side of the wall at a distance of one meter and a half. She looks at him but she doesn't come any nearer towards him. Little Filipp senses the painful distance. There is something inside her that is hurting her very much when she's trying to give (express) her love. The source of that something is originating from her own traumatic youth.

I interfere. I take Yvon to the side of the wall where little Filipp is standing. They fall in each other's arms. I let them fuse together till they become one loving whole (entity).

Post-control

I lost my sorrow! It feels good now. Very good!

February 8

Yesterday evening I spoke with Yvonne through the phone. My feelings were bothering me again. This time they were dominated by a panicky feeling that I'm losing her gradually.

Target-feeling

It's about the before mentioned feeling, somewhere in my throat. I'm concentrating on that feeling.

Image

I'm seeing an image. Little Filipp is on the beach with his grandmother and his mother. There are hundreds, maybe even thousands of people on the beach, but nobody is going into the water. It's too dangerous. There's a storm going on at sea. Swimming ban. Only a few brave people (or stupid attention-grabbers?) are going into the water to take a swim. My mother thinks of herself that she's an excellent swimmer, She goes into the water. Hundreds of people are watching. She's increasingly swimming away from the coastline and she's disappearing out of sight behind the extremely high waves. Little Filipp doesn't see her anymore. He's afraid that she's going to drown, that he's going to lose her forever and he starts panicking.

I interfere. I try to embrace little Filipp. It's no use. His view is focused on the point where his mother has disappeared behind the waves. He's so very tense, that he's totally unaware of my presence. His full attention is directed ad that specific point in the sea. I wonder what I could do to help him. Suddenly I know what to do. I hired a lifeboat, manned by two strong men, to sail alongside his mother. They're keeping an eye on her and they can intervene immediately if something should go wrong. Little Filipp sees the lifeboat accompanying his mother and he's getting a bit more quiet. I'm holding him in my arms. Unfortunately he's still tense and he's still worrying. He's still afraid to lose his mother. I'm thinking of something else to reassure him even more. I send for a helicopter. His mother is getting a broad belt which is being connected to a thick rope. With this rope the helicopter is being able to pull her out of the water in one jerk, exactly like a dog owner would pull his little dog out of the swimming pool with a leash. Under these circumstances his mother keeps on swimming. Little Filipp is seeing the helicopter and the lifeboat now. The knowledge that nothing bad could happen to his mother, is giving him a comforting feeling. His panic is disappearing. He's relaxing now, but nevertheless he keeps watching and waiting for his mother. After having been waiting for a long time, at last she's coming back totally exhausted. Little Filipp loves his mama very much. He embraces her and he never wants to release her anymore!

Back to the target-feeling

Little Filipp is lying on the coach. He's in distress. His mother doesn't want to console him. She doesn't take the least trouble to even try to. I interfere. I take him into my arms giving him a lot of love. We are going to our trauma-paradise. He's being taken care of by his grandmother. She gives him love. He relaxes and his distress is disappearing. I sit by and watch. I'm feeling a lot of distress. I say to my grandma that I can't manage to go on like this. I keep on bringing countless little Filipp's to this place. When is this finally going to stop? She embraces me. I cry and I feel her love and support. She tells me I'll have to keep carrying on.

Post-control

By now the feeling has been lowered under 10 percent.

February 9

Currently I'm involved in a medical examination for the benefit of my social security remittance. I already had a consultation with an insurance physician. This didn't went well. In his report he just ignored the most and the worst symptoms.

Insurance physicians are under high pressure. The government has issued a number of necessary financial cutbacks. That's why insurance physicians are trying out various tricks to prevent that clients might be going to be declared disabled (unable to work). In that case a remittance doesn't have to be paid, so another big saving has been realized. At the moment I'm anxiously waiting for the second consultation. I'd like to know what's the origin of my tension.

Target-feeling

I'm concentrating on the tension. Immediately I feel anxiety.

Image

I am (thirteen years old) at school and I'll have to fight another boy. I know that boy quite well and I know that he's a good person. Yet I'll have to fight him (though I have forgotten the reason why). I'm very afraid to hurt him, to damage him. I don't want to do that at all, because deep down inside he's a good and gentle boy and he never did me any harm. His name is Vladimir. I don't want to get hit either. I'm sure (convinced) that the very same counts for him. I interfere.

I let Filipp stand still. It's no use. Vladimir doesn't dare to hit now. He sees that Filipp has no intention to start a fight. Nevertheless he keeps challenging Filipp. I let Filipp sit quietly and I tell him to close his eyes. At this moment Vladimir doesn't know what to do anymore. He has become confused. After having been scolding a bit, he eventually leaves. It's settled now.

Back to the target-feeling.

Image

I see many pupils in the cloakroom of my school. Most of them are neither my friends, nor my enemies. They are the hanger-ons, who always stood watching and laughing when I was being pestered, belittled or intimidated.

The time has come for my payback. There are a few people in the cloakroom, who never participated in laughing at me. I like them. They're getting a protection suit with oxygen cylinders like rescue workers are using when confronted with dangerous substances. The doors are being closed......

Have you ever seen a big water cannon, which the fire brigade is using when fighting big fires? I've got one of those now. I took the far most biggest one! I point my canon on the hanger-ons and open the valve. The only difference is that instead of water, an enormous quantity of thin human shit (like diarrhea) is coming out of the canon under very high pressure. I'm squirting everyone from top to toe all over with this shit. I can hardly describe what a delicious feeling this gives me! Everywhere shit is flying around. After a few rounds I notice that some hanger-ons are beginning to get breathing problems. That doesn't surprise me at all, for meanwhile the school cloakroom has been overflowed with the shit. It's time to clean up. I close my canon. I allow the youngsters wearing the protection suits to leave the cloakroom through a door which had been sealed and shut tight. I'll have them squirted clean in a separate room. This time I'm using clean water. They're allowed to put out the security suits and come to me. I activate the sprinkler installation in the ceiling of the cloakroom. Out of the many tiny showers comes a lot of water which is rinsing the hanger-ons until they are clean again. They are all exhausted with fighting against the shit. I let them crawl away to the outside. They are so worn out, that they are immediately going to sit on the ground while some of them are even going to lie down. They are stinking terribly. I look at them and I can't help feeling a bit sorry for these "poor little souls". Nevertheless, they got what they deserved!

Post-control

What a marvellous feeling! I even don't feel tension anymore!

February 10

I notice that my trauma-handling is entering a new phase. Instead of heavy emotions, now I'm suffering a lot from feelings of anxiety and stress. Previously I wasn't aware of having that much stress and anxiety, because these feelings were shut out (pushed to the background) by strong emotions (like sorrow and anger). Literally as well as metaphorically, I'm very tired of my tensions, stress and unexplainable fears.

I'm in anticipation of my second consultation with the insurance physician. With mounting tension I check my postbox three times a day. I'm expecting an invitation for this consultation any time now. When I think about it, I'm feeling tension and anxiety.

Target-feeling

I'm concentrating on that anxiety.

Image

I'm seeing little Filipp, who is scared to death. His mother is having another tantrum (fit of anger). She's throwing everything she can get her hands on. She says: "I'm going to give such a bang on your head, that you'll never be able to stand up again!". Little Filipp is protecting his head because he's very afraid that she's going to hit his head with a random solid object. Little Filipp's nerves are at full strain in anticipation of the big smack on his head. He's feeling utterly unsafe and he fears for his life. I interfere. I wonder what he's needing at this very moment. Safety. I have his mother rolled up into a big thick pancake. I make a hole in front of her nose to make it possible for her to breath. The pancake is standing straight up in front of us. I have a large blue ribbonmbeing tied around the pancake. The mother is struggling against this treatment. Little Filipp is feeling a bit safer. However he's still afraid that she could be able to tear herself loose. I have the outside of the pancake being painted with melted sugar. The sugar is getting solid, as a result of which a hard cocoon comes into being. Little Filipp feels a bit safer now. However the image of the pancake-cocoon in the corner of the living room is not yet completely visible. He (little Filipp) is afraid that she still might be able to release herself. We make a chain and we fasten the pancake to the wall. This doesn't change little Filipp's feelings of fear for a bit. The pancake has to be removed from the house. We hang the pancake upside down on a hook above a river. Little Filipp and I are going to stand on a bridge, so we can look at the hanging pancake from a safe distance.mNow he (little Filipp) is finally feeling completely safe. His stress as well as his tension are disappearing. I take him into my arms and I bring him to our trauma-paradise.

Back to the target-feeling

My target-feeling has been diminished. But nevertheless there's still enough fear present. I'm concentrating on that subject.

Image

A new image is appearing. Little Filipp is swimming. By accident he has swallowed a lot of water. The water has also entered his nose. He's scared stiff. He's coughing. The water is coming out of his nose and mouth. Fortunately his grandmother is also on the beach. She takes him into her arms and she's trying to help him. She gives little Filipp something sweet to drink and he's slowly recuperating from his shock. I'll let it be at this.

Back to the target-feeling

Image

My grandmother has just passed away. It's 1987. I'm 10 years old. I keep repeating to myself: I'll never see her again. I'll never see her again. I'll never see her again. It causes distress. At the same time I see a view of her room where she's lying in her bed being terminally ill. Caused by the neuropathic pains in her face she has to suffer so terribly, that I'll be glad that she finally will be released from this ordeal. The indescribable severe neuropathic pains in her face could not be compared with the worst kind of toothache. There was no cure whatsoever to relieve these pains, because she was in the final stadium of cancer. Several times a day I heated in the oven a little linen sack filled with sand, which she held against her face almost constantly. That was the only way to ease the pain a little bit. Yet she was almost continuously moaning caused by the unbearable pains. I felt terribly sorry for her.

I'm dominated by a feeling of distress, mixed with a reassuring thought about her release from the pain. I'm mentally wasted. I'm filled with my own heavy emotions. I have no room for extra sorrow, which I feel for her. I can't manage it. The sorrow for her feels like a big block of concrete on the bottom of my soul. It's the kind of block which is being used for constructing the foundation of houses.

I interfere. I don't know exactly what to do. I only see the block of concrete somewhere below me. I'm making it smaller and smaller until it fits my hand.

Suddenly my mind transforms it to a souvenir. A teeny-weeny concrete little block made of gold! I wonder what I should do with it subsequently. I put it in my trouser pocket. I know that there's a hole in my trouser pocket and that sooner or later the souvenir is going to disappear through that hole by itself. I hope that it's going to fall unnoticed by me through the hole somewhere on the street or during a walk in the country side.

The coming days I'm going to watch my feelings for granny.

Post-control

Het target-feeling is now below 10 percent.

February 11

I'm furious. I'm receiving an email from a client of our foundation for the benefit of which I'm doing voluntary work. This client is a typical "nagging client". He's sending tens of emails, he doesn't bother at all to study and to use my explanation, he writes in a disparaging language and he keeps harping on to impose what he wants. It makes me furious! I'd rather give him a taste of his own medicine. I know that I'll have to remain being businesslike. However my anger is a great nuisance to me.

Target-feeling

My anger. I'm concentrating on it.

Image

Philippe is being dragged at his hairs across the ground by two men and after that he's being knocked down in a public toilet. One of them has a bald head and a powerful build. Somebody told me that he's a hard criminal and that he also has killed people during his "career". The other one is smaller, but he's very aggressive. Both of them are under the influence of drugs and alcohol. They are very violent as well as furious in their aggression. Philippe is being beaten and forced to hand over his money. I interfere. I take the men away from Philippe. I ask him what he needs. His answer is clear! A "baseball bat"! Philippe is furious because of the dreadful pain and the distress. He doesn't let the grass grow under his feet and immediately starts "working on" both men with his new aid. They are both lying on the ground now. The bald one is very afraid of dying. I can see that in his eyes. Philippe' s distress is diminishing but his anger isn't. He's still filled up with the adrenaline. Continuing the beating isn't going to take his anger away. Something else has to be invented. We hang them in a tree upside down. It doesn't change Philippe 's anger by no means. Then we put these two criminals in the middle of a basin belonging to a purification system, where the excrement of the whole city is coming together. There are turds floating everywhere on the surface. A view of two pitiful men in the middle of a bunch of shit causes that Philippe's anger is diminishing with 50 percent. There's still something left to be thought of, for the anger hasn't fully disappeared yet. We fasten them with their legs in a valve through which the excrement is continuously flushed. This view eventually seems to do the job. Philippe is laughing. His anger is decreasing quite a bit more, but it still isn't completely vanished. Next we cover both men with liquid cement and we let them dry up under the burning sun on a beach. Their clothes are getting hard owing to the cement. They can hardly move. Now they are sitting on their knees and they are begging to be released. There still is a little remainder of Philippe's anger left, which he wants to get rid of. He decides to shave the head of the second man bald as a keepsake. Then both heads are being thoroughly rubbed in with the shit. We let the shit dry up until it gets hard. They're now wearing wigs made of shit with very sharp edges. We have to laugh again. Now they are allowed to leave. My anger has finally vanished at last.

Back to the target-feeling

Image

A boy is standing on a stair-case and he's constantly spitting on Filipp (eleven years old). He's older, much taller and a lot stronger. Apart from that he's intimidating Filipp. Filipp is feeling powerless, sad and angry. I interfere. I ask Filipp what he needs. Just a "backup" he says. He wants to feel my presence behind his back. Now he feels that a grownup (I) is standing behind him to back him up. That gives him a lot of selfconfidence. At first he wanted to beat that boy, but he realizes that this isn't the proper way to handle. Instead Filipp turns the boy's arm behind his back and pushes his face into a big mound of dog shit. It helps a bit, but Filipp is not yet released from his anger. We're going to try something else. This time Filipp grabs his neck and pushes his face into a huge mountain of elephant shit. The mountain is that high that the boy is falling inside it. Now we can merely see his legs sticking out of the mountain. Filipp is laughing. The boy now has been forgiven. Let bygones be bygones.

Back to the target-feeling

Image

Little Filipp gets a rock-hard smack on his right ear. The pain is so heavy that he's feeling it somewhere in the middle of his head. He's screaming caused by the pain and he cries for his mama for protection. He's not going to get that protection from her. His mama was the one who gave him the smack. I interfere. We put mother in a big cage. We place this cage in a sea container which we lock up properly. I take little Filipp into my arms and I give him my love. He doesn't sense this love. He's only feeling terrible pain, which causes him to cry and scream. Slowly the pain is fading away. I take him with me to our trauma-paradise, where he's gradually recovering.

Back to the target-feeling

Filipp is 15 years old. He's got a new scooter. An older boy asks him for a ride to his house. Filipp is trusting and he brings him to his district. It appears to be a camp and it's not a safe place because of the criminals who are living there. The boy gets off the scooter, grabs the handlebars, pushes Filipp aside and it's obvious that he's trying to take away the scooter. Filipp is very afraid. His heart goes on the rampage. If this attempt should succeed, Filipp will never see his scooter back again. I interfere. I ask Filipp what he needs right now (at this very moment). He wants to feel me behind him. That gives him selfconfidence. He also wants the boxing glove with which he hits the boy, as a result of which he is blown away from the scooter. But Filipp's fear isn't disappearing. It's not the boy he's afraid of. Instead of him he really fears the grown up criminal brothers of the boy and their gang, who are always coming to take revenge for the benefit of their comrades. At this very moment they're all coming outside armed with knives, guns and clubs. Filipp wants a weapon. A big and a fast one. He picks and chooses an enormous machine gun, provided with fifty barrels which are solidly assembled together. This way a large number of shots can be fired at the same time. Filipp takes hold of that weapon and he starts firing right away. The metallic sound of fired bullets begins to fill the air. That causes a good feeling. The firepower of the weapon is unbelievable. Within a few seconds the whole gang is lying eliminated on the street. Their houses now look like colanders. Filipp ceases fire. It's dead silent all around. The older boy is still standing in front of Filipp's scooter. He's completely silent because of the things that happened before his eyes. His mouth stays open and he's scared to death of Filipp now. Eventually he's running away. Filipp is feeling fine now. He takes his scooter and he's slowly riding away.

Post-control

Back to the target-feeling

I don't feel anger for that "nagging client" anymore.

February 12

I'm taking my dachshunde out for an evening walk. The large dog belonging to the neighbours, is again walking around unleashed. Indeed, more than that. The owner is simply going with his dog in our direction, forcing us to get out of the way. I'm preparing ourselves for an attack of his dog. His dog is running rapidly growling toward us, ready to attack my little dachshunde, but at the very last moment he's being stopped by my neighbour. He's shouting at me: "Nothing is the matter!". I feel that I'm rapidly getting into a stressful situation. A month ago I wrote my neighbour a letter in which I politely asked him to take his dog for a walk while being leashed. I don't feel considered seriously They just ignored my concerns. I'm going to send a written complaint to the local authority, containing the below mentioned arguments.

Dear Sir / Madam,

I'm the owner of two little dogs (dachshunde). In the second half of December, together with my dogs, I have been attacked by a big dog owned by my neighbours right in front of the staircase of my own house. Their dog was not leashed. I was very shocked when this happened. I worried a lot about both the safety of my dogs and of my own. Afterwards I wrote a letter to my neighbours containing my friendly request to take their dog for a walk while being properly leashed. My neighbours didn't react to my letter. You'll find a copy of this litter in the attachment. Much to my regret my request has not been taken seriously. Their dog is still being taken out for a walk without being leashed. In the evening of February 11th, together with my dogs I have once more been confronted with the unleashed dog of my neighbours.

In the evenings I don't feel safe anymore in my own street. Every time I leave my own house, I'm looking around at full strain whether the big dog of the neighbours is walking around unleashed. I consider this as being very annoying. It's a great nuisance to me. According to the rules of the local authority for dog owners, one is compelled to take his/her dog for a walk in the built up area while being leashed. This rule is not being complied with by our neighbours.

I herewith kindly request you to consult with the owner of the dog about his legal responsibility and to inform me about the result of this communication as soon as possible.

Attachment: a copy of my (above mentioned) letter to my neighbours

We look forward to receiving your reply.

Yours sincerely,

Philippe Izmailov

What am I sensing now? The last time when (that) his dog attacked us, I felt completely overwhelmed by my anger, stress and grief. Normally stress and anger would cause me to walk up and down my living room now. At this moment things are different. Almost nothing (hardly anything) is bothering me. Nevertheless I'm feeling some emotions, which are still bottled up somewhere in my throat, seeking their way out. A nice opportunity to do a trauma-meditation.

Target-feeling

A feeling in my throat. It's not quite clear for me what it's trying to indicate. It's restless. It appears to be distress, stress and anger. I'm concentrating on these possible symptoms.

Image

I'm feeling pain on the right side of my face. That pain is caused by a slap, that someone gave me. The slap must have been that hard, that I'm feeling the effect of it on my skull. I'm not getting any image at all. I even cannot remember who did it and when this person did it. I'm only feeling the pain caused by the slap. I'm concentrating on that pain. Gradually the image starts to shape an outline. I'm thirteen years old. I went fishing with a friend on a remote peninsula. Suddenly we're getting company. A group of young men who are going to extort money from us. My friend manages to escape. I get a hard slap on my face. One of them challenges Filipp. He's intimidating Filipp, hoping that he's going to attack him. Then they would have a motive to beat him up together. Filipp is boiling with rage, but he can't do a thing. They want money and he hasn't got any money. I interfere and ask Filipp what he needs now. He wants to fight the men one after another. I'm keeping everyone at a distance. This time Filipp doesn't want any means. He's so furious that he beats the first man completely to pieces. One after another all four men are lying on the ground. They want to stand up and attack altogether at the same time. Filipp wants a baseball bat. With that aid he's handling his enemies the hardest possible way. After the beating they're being buried in the sand up till their necks. Their heads are being totally shaved and their bald heads are being rubbed in with shit. After that Filipp is letting their heads dry up. They look like four big chocolate balls. Filipp can't help laughing. His anger has decreased. They're afraid now and we set them free. They immediately are going to run for it, except one of the men. He returns the belongings of Filipp and he apologies. He's very afraid. Then he also runs away like a beaten dog with his tail between his legs. Filipp is not yet completely finished with them. We get in a military helicopter and we're going to hunt for them. We're flying over the wood where we can see the men on the ground running away. There still is a slight remainder of anger for these men, which Filipp has to get rid off. He's shooting at the fleeing men with big elephant turds, which are fired from the canons of our helicopter.

The turds are so big, that the men one by one are disappearing into a mountain of shit. The only parts of them which are still visible are either their legs or their hands. They're clumsily trying to free themselves. It provides a fantastic sight. We let them go now.

Back to the target-feeling

Image

I see an image. Philippe is about eighteen years old. He is on a remote part of a beach, where hardly nobody is present. A number of metres further on a few adolescents are being extorted by two big fat men. First they are forced to give their food to them and then more and more. Their way of speaking (linguistic usage) indicates their criminal backgrounds. Filipp feels sorry for these boys. He's furious, but he's feeling completely powerless. If he's going to interfere, he'll become a victim just like the boys. I decide to interfere myself. I ask Filipp what he's needing right now. A baseball bat! Filipp is very angry. He knocks the living daylights out of the fat men. They're now lying on the ground. We fetch a speedboat, we fasten their legs to the boat with ropes and we're going to sail with the highest possible speed. Both men are being dragged along in the wake of the speedboat. I doesn't yield the desired result. It doesn't change the way Filipp is feeling. Something else has to be thought of (invented). We put them back on the beach, we pull their underpants down, we put fireworks in their assholes and light it. Then we let them go, their back parts being on fire. They're running away. Everybody is laughing at them. Filipp's anger is decreasing , but it isn't completely vanished yet. We get into our helicopter and we go hunting. This time we have attached two enormous bags on the underside of our helicopter. The fire brigade is using these bags to do their job in case of big forest fires. They fill the bags with water, they fly over the fire and they're pouring the water on the fire. Because the backsides of our "friends" are on fire, we think it seems to be good idea not to go shooting this time. Our intentions definitely differ from those of the fire brigade and we fill the bags with thin shit instead of water. Equipped with this we're going hunting. We're flying above the forest. We have no trouble to track down our "friends". The smoke coming out of their backsides is rising above the trees. Solemnly we open the bags one by one on top of our "friends". A marvellous feeling of being released from my anger is filling my chest.

February 15

I received a letter from my mother. The letter is over-loaded with humiliations, intimidations, accusations, blackmail and terms of abuse. While reading, at first I'm feeling the anger. Afterwards my anger is gradually diminishing and from the depth of my chest the sorrow is coming forward.

Target-feeling

My sorrow is located in my chest and in my throat. I'm concentrating on both.

Image

I'm seeing little Filipp. His mother is beating him and she's yelling at him. She is furious and very aggressive. Her words are even worse than her slaps. Little Filipp is crying and he's begging for mercy. Each word from her hits like a smack. He's feeling a lot of pain inside his mind and body. He loves her very much, he's very much in distress.

I interfere. The mother is being tied up, so that she cannot beat little Filipp. Her mouth is being taped, so that her verbal aggression can't be heard anymore. I take little Filipp in my arms. I feel his distress. He loves his mother very much. In response to his love he's getting her aggression and anger in return. He doesn't understand why. This increases his distress. I'm giving him my loving care. When he's falling asleep, I take him with me to my trauma-paradise.

Back to the target-feeling

Image

I'm 30 years old. I'm living in the Netherlands for a few years now. My mother has come to visit. We arrive at the front door of my girlfriend. There is an argument going on between me and my mother. She pushes through to get what she wants, like it has always been the case. I refuse to submit to her whims. She gets a tantrum (fit of anger). She beats me on the head with a bottle filled with water. I'm lucky that at this very moment she hasn't got something heavier at her disposal. Once that used to be a hammer, with which she wanted to hit me on the head. She's behaving just like the time when I still was a helpless little child and she could do to me everything she wanted to, without being punished. I'm infuriated caused by her behaviour and by the pain in my head. I grab her with my hands and I pull her inside. I'm looking straight into her eyes. I'm shouting at the top of my voice: "That's enough! I'm NOT a little child ANYMORE, whom you can beat and abuse without being punished". I'm hearing Yvonne, my girlfriend, yelling on the background. She's in a panic. She's very afraid and she shouts at me to release my mother! I ask Yvonne to go and book a return ticket for my mother immediately. I want my mother to leave today. That's the way it happened. In anticipation of her flight, we took my mother to my apartment, where she cut the pictures of my childhood to little pieces, she ransacked my house completely and she took a number of my belongings without having asked for it. Yvonne finally took my mother to the airport, where she boarded her plane to Russia.

I'm seeing an image of myself and my mother in the living room of Yvonne. I feel terrible. My mother hasn't learned a thing during the past years and she hasn't changed whatsoever. This hurts me tremendously and causes a lot of distress within me. I don't want to see her anymore. I want to have her out of the way as soon as possible. I intervene. I take Philippe aside and I embrace him. He's completely numb with nerves. He's in a state of shock, but he doesn't realize it. He's only feeling anger and a lot of distress. In the image I send for a Mail-van. The van takes my mother along right away. She's going to be a package with destination Russia. I'm holding Philippe until he recovers. I take him with me to our trauma-paradise.

Back to the target-feeling

Image

Philippe is 19 to 20 years old. He's breadwinner. Like many jobless youngsters (there were hardly any jobs at that time) he's driving around in his old car, hoping to give someone a lift for a small fee. So you could regard this as some kind of cab driving. At home he provides his mother with money to be able to buy food. However the situation with regard to public transport in the city went through a drastic change. A new kind of public transport was introduced, consisting of small rapid vans intended for a maximum of ten passengers, who were allowed to stop anywhere out of reach of the bus stops. From that moment on voyagers are allowed to get in or out everywhere they prefer to. This development has made my "lift services" needless. Getting clients is getting more and more difficult, not to say almost impossible. Driving around is almost useless and only costs a lot of fuel. I decide to take a position near the airport, where I can wait for arriving passengers. The local "cab-gang" has occupied this area. There exists a heavy competition. Gang members have stabbed two tires of my car when I was looking for clients at the airport. There are no other jobs because of the large unemployment. At home I'm constantly told that we have no money and that I should make more working hours. I'm under great pressure. On the one hand I have no clients, which means no income. On the other hand there is the emotional pressure practiced by my mother. I'm feeling highly responsible for our family (being my mother and myself). After the downfall of the Soviet Union, the economy of Russia collapsed during the nineties. There simply are no other jobs whatsoever in the city. Suddenly something is crossing my path. A fellow student from the university where I was studying, asked me if I would be skillful enough to reassemble the engine of his broken down car. I'm well aware of the money pressure at home and my responsibility for the family. Reluctantly I accept this order. The engine had been removed from his car and was in a completely dismantled situation. We agreed on a small fee (between friends). I reassembled the engine. However, because I lacked sufficient experience with regard to repairing that type of car, I made a fatal mistake. After the first start the engine immediately got jammed. The engine parts couldn't be restored, because in the past they already had been restored several times. About this fact my fellow student has lied to me emphatically. I had explicitly asked him about possible restored parts in the past before I started the reassembling job. I could have paid for a restoration, but that wasn't possible anymore. New engine parts cost a fortune. I had an argument with that fellow student. I proposed to share the costs of new engine parts between the two of us. He refused. He has brought in criminals from the local mafia. They started threatening and extorting me (I already attended to this in another trauma-meditation). To settle this situation my mother suddenly produced a lot of money. It appeared that she has systematically put aside a certain amount of the money which I had been earning during my taxi driving period and which I had given her to go on errands. This happened behind my back. If I had known that we still had money to our disposal, I would never have accepted that reassembling job. In fact she has been lying about the financial situation at home all the time. I felt betrayed and deceived by my own mother.

I intervene. I ask what Filipp needs now. He wants to have a talk with his mother. He wants to get rid of his emotions and he wants her to listen to him. I put the mother in front of Filipp. He starts to talk about his feelings. The mother is smiling, isn't listening and eventually she turns her back to him. She doesn't take him seriously. I intervene again. I let the mother appear before the court. The court is going to judge her by her behaviour. Filipp is allowed to come forward and to try to express his feelings again. The mother is sitting on the chair which is intended for persons who are being interrogated. She's smiling and she's still not listening. The judge tells her that he wants her to take the feelings of Filipp seriously now and to do her utmost to listen to him. She does so reluctantly. Filipp opens his heart and he tells about the way he's feeling. He tells about his sorrow and his pain, adding that he feels deceived and betrayed. The mother denies it all. She says that all this is made up utter nonsense and she starts to curse. The judge strikes with his hammer on the table and asks her urgently to hold her tongue. She obeys. The judge calls for a witness. The large doors behind the public are being opened and closed again. There's nobody to be seen. A few moments later a little child is coming forward. It's the five years old little Filipp, who just entered the courtroom. Because he's so little, we couldn't recognize him among the public. He's looking bad. He has blue bags under his eyes and he's awfully distressed caused by the things his mother did to him. His mother is looking down at little Filipp in a disparaging way. He's a classic example of a living evidence. The judge confronts her with this. The mother is becoming furious and aggressive. She wants to attack little Filipp. Filipp takes him into his arms to protect him. Two policemen are stopping the berserk gone mother and are pushing her back into the chair. The judge asks me if I still want to say something. Filipp asks his mother: "Why do you hate me so badly? I want to understand" She's getting angry again. Trogs full of reproaches are thrown all over Filipp. It's obvious for everyone in the courtroom that these reproaches are directed at (meant for) her ex-husband. The judge says: "This isn't your husband! This is your son! Are you aware of that? ". She doesn't respond to this remark. It seems as if she has lost all contact with reality and is now only involved in cultivating her feelings of hate and anger. She doesn't sense any difference at all between reality (her son) and her ex-husband.. She's still very angry and she's continuing throwing blames around. Right now I'm sensing very clearly the begging for love by little Filipp and the aggression of our mother. Little Filipp is very afraid. Everybody is looking at Filipp and little Filipp in silence. The judge says that it's better if I, the grown-up Philippe, am going to take care of little Filipp from now on. I'll do that. I look at my mother and I realize that mentally she's gravely ill.

February, 15

I received a businesslike e-mail with an angry content from a certain person. This person has given a judgment on our product in the local newspaper in the past. Because the judgment was favourable, I published the newspaper article on our website. In addition to the judgment I also published the name of the person in question on our website including his photograph. Exactly as some other websites did with the same article from the same newspaper. So it happened, that six months later I suddenly received an e-mail from the person in question. He claims that he didn't grant his permission to publish his judgment as well as his photograph on our website. He also claims that his name is being "misused" and he's threatening to take legal steps. Although I know that from a legal point of view I'm having every right to do what I did, I'm offering my apologies, because I understand and respect the feelings of this person. During a consultation by telephone I settled this matter with him to our mutual satisfaction. Nevertheless this incident evoked a huge feeling of agitation within me. When I'm paying attention to this feeling, I'm sensing an enormous anxiety, which is rising somewhere from the inside of my belly and which is looking for expression through my throat.

174

Target-feeling

The anxiety in my belly. I'm concentrating on that.

Image

I'm seeing a very little Filipp, no more than four years old. He's alone in the dark. It's spooky all around him. He's afraid of a witch and ghosts, who are flying around him. He's afraid of the unknown. Little Filipp is thinking of something horrible, that might be going to happen to him now. I interfere. I take little Filipp in my arms. He's feeling a lot safer at once. I put on the big light. We're standing in the middle of a large gym. It doesn't feel pleasant in here. I wonder what little Filipp is needing now. The witch! She's still alive! I let her appear at once. She arrives and she's flying around us. I take hold of a sword and I chop her to little pieces. This helps. His fear is decreasing, but he's still afraid that she might be coming back to life. He's right. I see a finger on her chopped off hand still moving! I collect all her leftovers, put them in a waste container and lock the cover. Afterwards I immediately send for a garbage lorry and I let the container be removed. Little Filipp isn't afraid any more. I take him with me to the trauma-paradise.

Back to the target-feeling

Image

Not so long ago little Filipp has learned to walk. He's now walking next to his mother. A big dog is attacking him, which frightens him tremendously and he's hiding behind his mother. The dog is immediately being stopped. Little Filipp only got scared stiff. He was afraid of the unknown and of what the dog could do to him. I interfere. I take little Filipp in my arms and I'm giving him my protection. I leash that dog and I give him/her to a bicyclist, who's taking him/her along. He disappears from (out of) the image. Little Filipp is getting quiet. I take him with me to our trauma-paradise.

Back to the trauma-feeling.

Image

Little Filipp is 7 years old. He and his mother are in the middle of a forest during a trip organized by his mother's employer. All participants want music. The driver of the rented bus walks to his vehicle to get some musicasettes. Little Filipp runs after him to get a bottle of water from the bus. The driver gets into the bus at the left side and extends his hand to pick up a musicassette. Because the cassette is lying in the opposite corner of the dashboard, which is still far away from the driver's hand, little Filipp wants to help him by picking it up and give it to the driver. I still don't know why, but the driver suddenly gives a hard slap on his hand. Little Filipp is very frightened by this unexpected reaction. His hand hurts. He runs away but he doesn't dare to tell his mother what happened. He's afraid that his mother is going to get angry at the driver. Little Filipp is confused, unsure and distressed. He has been punished by an unknown man without a reason. It's not fair! I interfere. I see to it that little Filipp is yet going to tell his mother about this event. She gets angry at the driver. She goes to him and starts abusing him. He says something in return, after which she starts beating him. The company trip has been spoilt. The worst part of it is that it doesn't change a thing in the way little Filipp is feeling. I'm going to do it differently now. I'm going back to the moment on which the driver was handing out the slap. On the last moment I pull little Filipp's hand away and I put a glowing red-hot frying pan instead of his hand. The driver slaps hard on the pan and he severely burns his hand. We can hear this very distinctly. This causes the desired effect. Little Filipp feels that now the injustice has been leveled.

Back to the target-feeling.

Image

Little Filipp loves his mama and he wants to do something nice for her. Pancakes are the most tasty delicacies one can eat, isn't it? "They sure are !", little Filipp considers. "It's decided!". He's going to bake pancakes for his mama. No sooner said than done. Mama is back from her work and she is very angry. The kitchen is a mess. The baking of the pancakes went wrong. Little

Filipp is standing in the middle of this heap of rubble and he's crying with distress. It's not fair! He meant well and now he's being punished in return. I interfere. I put the mother under a cold shower. I see to it that she's not going to be able to relax in there. Little Filipp is feeling a lot safer now. I quickly clean the kitchen. It's shining all over the place now. I'm comfortng little Filipp and I'm giving him a lot of loving care. Then I take him with me to our trauma-paradise.

Back to the target-feeling.

Image

Filipp is 14 years old. His mother is doing the cooking on our veranda. There is an argument going on between the two of them, which is rapidly developing into a tremendous outburst of rage. The mother grabs a large kitchen knife and flings it at Filipp. The knife flies a few centimetres past his body and finally gets stuck in the ground. Caused by the shock, his nervous system is getting stiff all over. He's paralysed with fear. He's running away. A few hours later, when his mother's rage has decreased, Filipp comes back. He asks her quietly if she realizes, that he could have been dead by now. She's looking straight into his eyes and says, her face being full of hatred: I PUT YOU INTO THIS WORLD AND I HAVE EVERY RIGHT TO FINISH YOU OFF! She means it. She adds to this, that he's the one to blame for what happened. He's shocked by her reaction and he's feeling powerless and unsafe. He doesn't understand why she hates him that much. That same evening his mother has an accident. She lets a lid of the hatch in the floor fall on her fingers, causing them to get jammed between the hatch and the gap. She's crying in severe pain. Filipp and his mother are together in a little country house with nobody else in the near vicinity. It's pitch-dark. Filipp is afraid that his mother is going to stab him to death while he's sleeping. I interfere. I ask what Filipp is mostly needing right now and I get his answer straightaway. I send for an ambulance. They examine the fingers of the mother and they take her with them. We close all doors and windows and lock them adequately. Filipp is feeling secure now. I take care of adequate lighting in the room where we're sitting at this very moment. I'm staying at his side. I'm embracing him. His sorrow and tension are now coming to the surface and he starts crying. When he has recovered himself, I take him with me to our trauma-paradise where he's being welcomed by numerous little Filipp's and by his grandmother. He's feeling at home now.

Back to the target-feeling

Image

It's December 31, New Year's Eve. Filipp is 13 years old. His mother orders him to open a bottle of champagne. Accidentally the cork is shooting out of the bottle with a lot of power and crushes a window in the kitchen. I see thick cracks in the window. The mother is angry, she's blaming the accident on Filipp. Filipp feels sad. It's not fair what his mother is doing now. I interfere. I put the mother under a cold shower. I installl a new window. I embrace Filipp and take him with me to our trauma-paradise.

February 25

A few months ago I applied for a sickness benefit. Last week I finally got a rejection. My mental pains, sufferings, trauma's and distresses have not been admitted, just like my psychological and physical complaints, which keep me awake at night time and which cause intense fatigue, headaches and sleepiness during the daytime. The insurance physician in fact has been handling the same judgment-method, as the one which has always been favored by my mother. That's the way I'm feeling it. My emotions were utter nonsense. My "imaginations", like she always called them. I had to quit that rubbish and I should start doing something "useful". In fact the reason of the rejection in both cases is indeed exactly based on the very same stupid arguments. Stop nagging, start doing something that makes sense! I can imagine that other people, being in my situation, are feeling misunderstood, neglected and rejected. They're getting indifferent and they are ending up in a victim 's role, where they're doomed to stay at least for a couple of years. This takes them even further away from their recovery and from the labor market.

The rejection did a lot to me. Something with huge emotional dimensions has been awakened inside me. A kind of mixture between heavy distress and deep mourning. Mentally and physically I'm feeling paralysed. I'm being totally beaten up to pieces. I don't like anything anymore. I have become completely indifferent with regard to everything around me. After having been in this situation for a week, I eventually manage to motivate myself to go meditating.

Target-feeling

The feeling in my throat.

Image

I'm seeing an image. Little Filipp, not more than five years old, is sitting on the floor among his toys. I hear his mother. She's furious and aggressive. She's yelling at him. He has to tidy up his toys. He's getting slaps on his head. It hurts and it causes al lot of distress. He doesn't understand why his mother is reacting at him in such a heartless and aggressive way. Because he loves her!.

I interfere. I put the mother behind a glass wall. I take little Filipp in my arms and I'm giving him a lot of loving care. I tidy his toys up in a big cardboard box. The box is not, as usual, placed in the corner of the living room. The mother is still being furious. I send for an ambulance. Two ambulance male nurses take her with them. I take little Filipp with me to our trauma-paradise. He sees his grandmother, runs towards her and he's falling into her arms. He starts to cry loudly. This time caused by the mental pain and his sorrow. He's yelling out of the depth of his belly because of his love distress. Little Filipp loves his mother so much. He doesn't understand why his mother is behaving as she does. She is loveless and she's just hurting him. Grandma is holding him, is giving him loving care and looks at me. We understand each other without having to use words. He's still too young to understand. He's slowly recovering. All children are gathering around the grandmother to have a look at the newcomer. They're feeling his pain and are feeling sorry for him. They're waiting. Little Filipp is fiercely clinging to the dress of his grandmother. That gives him a sense of security. He's looking around. Suddenly his belly is going to gurgle and he lets go of a loud burp. Everybody is in stitches. The ice has been broken. Now they're going to play together.

Back to the target-feeling

Image

Little Filipp is again being beaten by his mother. She's yelling at him. I'm going to deal with this trauma in the same way.

182

Back to the target-feeling

Image

Filipp is going through his puberty. The mother is suddenly getting angry and very aggressive. She's attacking Filipp. He's being beaten. Her verbal violence is even worse than the blows. Trays filled with her hate are coming towards Filipp. She says that she would gladly finish him off. Her fits are gone. I'm going to send for an ambulance with male nurses to take her away. I see Filipp sitting on the couch in his room. Mentally he's totally broken up and he's paralyzed caused by shock. On the inside he's feeling a lot more dead than alive. He's not crying. I'm going to sit next to him. I try to embrace him. His body feels like a flattened steak. It's weak all over without any energy left. The life in his body seems to have ceased to exist. (It feels exactly like my situation during the first week after the rejection of my application for a sickness benefit). He says: "If she doesn't love me, what's the use for me to still being alive? She's the only one I've got and whom I love. There's nobody else in my life". I'm keeping my arms around him. I'm telling him that his mother is very sick. She's not being able to express her love because she's very much entangled with herself. Deep inside her exists a little girl who does love you. This girl has been hidden so deeply, that she's never going to get the chance to express her love. I keep holding Filipp in my hands. We keep sitting on the couch for quite a long time. I decide to take him with me to our trauma-paradise. There he sees his

183

grandmother, he falls into her arms and he starts crying. Grandma comforts him, gives him her loving care and she says that his mama is sick. It still lasts quite a long time before he finally starts recovering.

February 28

For many years now I have been hiding my mother's letters in a box, far away from my eyes and my feelings. I had been reading many of these letters rapidly and superficially when they arrived. It would cause too much pain, stress and anxiety for me to study her letters thoroughly. Every time when a letter from her arrived, my body got a shock reaction. I was petrified with nerves and at the same time I got paralyzed with fear as if I was standing in front of a lion. My legs got weak en my hands started to tremble from the tension. This was my response to her letters.

Now her letters are lying before me. I have bound all of them together with a rubber band. I don't dare to read them yet. That would still be s a step too fast (big). I'm sensing an enormous feeling of distress coming up in my throat. I'm going to meditate on that feeling.

Target-feeling

The feeling of distress in my throat. I'm concentrating on it.

Image

The first time no traumatic events from my past are penetrating my consciousness. I hear myself calling: "Mama, Mama, I miss you so!". I'm feeling a lot of love for her and I'm not capable to express this loving feelings. I can't embrace her, I can't give her a kiss and I can't tell her how much I love her. Instead I'm doing my utmost to keep her at a large distance from me and from my life. (Now I'm feeling that I have access to hidden feelings. I get up and I'm going to sit at my computer). I have changed my phone number as well as my email address, because I didn't want to be terrorized by her. I also didn't give her the address of my new place of residence. She's sending her letters to the address of my girlfriend's stepfather. I arranged it this way because I'm afraid that my mother is standing at my front door all of a sudden and could be going to manipulate me once again. I restrict myself to sending her as few letters as possible. I also keep my scarce letters to her very short, because I know that all information which I give to her, is being used against me. I know that my mother is extremely capable of manipulating people. A few years ago I tried to break off the contact with her. At that time I was already living in the Netherlands. She phoned me every week and each time, she held a monologue, which lasted for exactly one minute sharp, during which she spit out her frustrations and anger over me, belittled and intimidated me, and each time she left me with a lousy feeling (saying: "It's YOUR fault, Philippe, that I (mother) is feeling so rotten! You're a bad son. You don't listen to mama!"). Before I had a chance to say something in return, she hung up. Each time this happened, I was in a shock and each time it took a week before I had recovered from this shock. Then after a week she phoned again and the same circus started all over again.

After a few months, I couldn't handle this anymore. I then cut my sim card in half and I took a new telephone number. Her letters were full of hate and accusations. I ruined her life, I'm a wicked son and I'm to blame for all this. This is a brief summary of the contents of her letters. I decided to stop writing her and to have no more contact whatsoever with her. I also informed her about my decision. After a few years I suddenly became an email from the Dutch consulate in Saint Petersburg:

Good morning, Sir!

This morning your mother, Violetta Izmailova, has paid a visit to the visa department of the Consulate General of the Netherlands in St. Petersburg and asked us to help her as she lost every contact with you. This is her new mobile-number. Please contact your mother as soon as possible.

All the best,

Consulate General of the Netherlands

I answered this letter from the Consulate as follows.

Dear Sir/Madam

I have not had contact with my mother for a couple of years due to a reason. My mother used to abuse me when I was a child. Nowadays I'm still suffering from a lot of psychological problems, which are caused during my childhood and for which I'm still undergoing therapy. My mother has broken off all contacts with me several times in the past. I do not want to have any contact with my mother and she's aware of that. So I herewith ask you to please stop helping her to look for me.

Kindest regards,

Philippe Izmailov

Six months later I got a phone call from a agent of the Dutch police force, confronting me with the following problem. He told me: "Philippe, don't be shocked. There's a letter from your mother lying before me. She asks us to give her your adress. I don't know what to do about this. I have never before experienced such a case! We're not allowed to give her your adress. What do you want me to do with her letter?" At that moment I really understood that my mother is capable to do everything to get me back into her grip. I then wrote a letter to her. She wrote me back that she had been terribly afraid that she had lost me. Since that time I occasionally send her a card, but I keep the writing limited. I keep her at a long distance from my life and my feelings. That has to be done in favour of my own self-protection.

Meanwhile I know that, apart from Borderline (Personality Disorder), my mother is also suffering from a bouquet of other personality disturbances. I can't communicate with my mother. She isn't listening. According to her, my feelings are utter nonsense and moreover they are based on imaginations. Usually she couldn't remember my trauma's. "Don't invent nonsense", she always said. When occasionally she could remember my trauma's, she always blamed me for it. She's always right. I'm not being able to communicate with my mother. I'm also not being able to change my mother. I'm feeling helpless. She's continuously playing with my feelings. She has been abusing my love for her countless times! My love has turned into my pain. Now I'm feeling a lot of distress. I'm feeling guilty for my own measures, which I took out of self- protection.

The cocktail containing pain, distress, powerlessness and my love (for her) is a very difficult combination. In this combination love is functioning as fuel for the feelings of pain, distress an powerlessness. They're constantly being nourished with my love for my mother. The unconditional love of a child for his/her mother has been anchored in human nature. This love is inexhaustible and can't be eliminated. This love provokes a chain reaction of pain, distress and powerlessness inside me. A number of times I succeeded to stop this chain reaction. I did this by locking up my love behind the bars of my anger. I confined my love. Closing off the fuel supply stops the chain-reaction. In that case temporary I'm feeling no pain, distress and powerlessness. Blocking one feeling by means of another, causes a lot of tension in my body as well as in my subconsciousness. At the same time the pressure on the kettle is becoming that high, that my emotions are going to look for a way out both in my dreams and in my various reaction patterns. In different area's such as businesslike communication, my relationship or social connections, I use to react too often out of my emotions (anger, sorrow etc.). This is causing disruption of contacts and large tensions in my mind and body. My subconsciousness is overloaded. I use to dream a lot, I sleep badly and I'm increasingly feeling tired. The love feelings have to be liberated. I'll have to find a way to be able to express my love without giving my mother the opportunity to start manipulating my feelings all over again. I'm going to express my love by putting it in writing.

The letter to my mother.

Dear mama. When I'm feeling my love for you, at the same time I experience feelings of sorrow. Love without sorrow doesn't exist anymore. I would gladly like to embrace you, but I can't. I've been suffering too much pain in the past, which restrains me from embracing you now. You'll be very surprised now reading this. "What pain? What in the name of God is he talking about? That's what you're thinking. I understand that. You're living in your own dream world, which is just next to the world of reality.

Sometimes they touch each other and then you're able to remember some events.

I know out of my experience, that it's no use to explain to you what's the origin of my pain and sorrow. That's why I restrict myself to telling you that the reason should be sought in the things that happened during my youth. You'll not be able to understand this. Again you'll be surprised, because you're convinced that you always have been a good mother. I'm not going to judge you on this. I'll try to convince myself that your behaviour is caused by your mental illnesses. Once again you'll be surprised. What is he talking about? That's what you're thinking now. I know that you consider yourself an intelligent woman. Many events have been erased from your memory and other events are not welcome in your memory. I'll not be able to reach you with my pain, sorrow and love. I'm not capable to explain it to you and you're never going to understand it, because you'll never be able to feel it and consequently to get down to the very heart of the matter. It's not because you don't want to, but it's because you cannot manage this. The borders of your world are heavily guarded. I cannot enter your world. Since I was born, I'm feeling an enormous emotional distance between the two of us, which still kept increasing as I was growing up. I'm not allowed to access to your feelings. Nobody is allowed to do so, including you yourself. I cannot feel any love coming from you. It's hurting me and it's causing me a lot of sorrow. I love you. I realize that the time we spent together on this earth is almost over. You're now 72 years old and your life time is restricted. I'm feeling that I'm gradually being losing you. It's a very painful process. I'm feeling powerless and very sad. There's a fair chance that I'm never going to see you again. I'm mourning, how strange as it may seem because you're still alive. I'm feeling guilty for not having been able to save you from your illness. I just don't know how to do that. I'm crying now. For years and years I wasn't able to cry because of you. I have been deeply hiding my pain and love for many years. I would be glad to be able to exchange the rest of my life for a few years of living happily together with you. I love you. Please forgive me, I'm begging you to do so.

I'll keep loving you forever.

Your son.

After all those years I finally managed to put my feelings in writing. I'm aware of the fact that THIS is the end. That's it! The story is over! Measured in time, her death is a postponed fact. Right now I'm feeling as if I wrote a farewell letter. God, what's happening in my mind now!?

February 29

I'm feeling sorrow. I know the sorrow is about my mother. The last few years I did my utmost to stay angry at my mother. My anger used to block my love. Because of my anger I felt no love for my mother. After my trauma-meditation my anger weakened and it has been replaced by the real feeling, which wasn't allowed to be felt before. I'm feeling love and sorrow. These are two sides of one medal. They're going through life together. The sorrow is caused by the distance between us, my powerlessness with regard to her illness and my love, which I'm not being able to express. I decide not to walk away any more from my sorrow and my love, nor to deny them or to hide them. I'm going to feel the love for my mother every day again. And by this I mean as intensely as possible! I realize that this is impossible without feeling my sorrow at the same time. For the time being, next to my love, my sorrow will be part of my feelings to a great extent. My sorrow is allowed to be felt. Right now my sorrow is still taking the very first place and it's leaving but a minor piece of space for my love. Somewhere inside my mind I know that the proportion between love and sorrow eventually will ever be changed. I just need to allow myself to feel love and sorrow every day over and over again! No matter how painful this may be. There has to be something for me to do to be able to ease the distance between us and my powerlessness. I can't change my mother. The only way to communicate with her about my feelings in a safe manner, is writing letters to her. All other options (talking in private, by telephone or writing by email), which I tried several times, have only caused manipulations, blackmail and even more pain. My mother isn't capable to hold conversations about feelings. She has no empathy, feels no pity, let alone compassion. Moreover she's not able to listen to other people. I'm going to write to her. As often as possible!

How I am changed

Like you have noticed while reading this book, I have been thoroughly cleaning up my "Flying Dutchman". Just like the count of Monte-Cristo I succeeded in escaping the prison of my nasty emotions. I left behind many of my Philippe-reactions once and for all. I'm feeling a lot lighter as before. I'm feeling relieved. I lost the biggest part of my luggage. I'm sensing inner space and rest inside myself again. I'm feeling joy. When this inner space is getting empty again, it will be automatically filled up with other positive emotions.

In my youth I got excited by the music of Bon Jovi, Roxette and Celine Dion. I could literally feel their music in my veins. On a certain moment this wasn't possible for me anymore. For many years I couldn't enjoy my favourite music anymore. It has ceased touching me. Luckily my nice emotions have returned. When I hear their music now, my emotions immediately are going to join the music, just like a couple of guitar strings.

Do's and don'ts of trauma-meditation

Please thoroughly read this chapter before you're going to start practicing a trauma-meditation. You ought to consult a specialist before deciding to start with Mindfulness Based Trauma Treatment. The advices and techniques which are taken down in this book might not be appropriate (suitable) for your specific situation.

In any case, before you're going to start, you should construct a mechanism of "the trauma-catapult" for the benefit of the protection of your own mind.

> ➤ The trauma-catapult is just like an ejection seat, which is catapulting the pilot out of the crashing plane. It's quickly taking your mind to safety. What is the function of the trauma-catapult during the trauma-meditation? The trauma-catapult is an experience from your past, which evokes an extremely strong positive emotion inside you. Think of an experience, which is causing you to laugh in stitches. You'll have to laugh so much, that your eyes are going to be filled with tears or that you even have to go for a pee. This extremely strong positive emotion is going to catapult you like an ejection seat out of the undergoing of your traumatic experience. My trauma-catapult has caused a situation at high school. I was following the lesson together with a classmate. Our teacher was in rage about the conduct of some pupils during the lesson.

She was yelling. Because she was being that angry, everyone in the classroom was silent. It was so silent that you could even hear a mosquito flying around in the classroom. Exactly on that very inconvenient moment, I started having the giggles. I did my utmost to hold my breath, which you could clearly see on my face. My classmate saw my suffering face and he also started having the giggles, which he tried to suppress. He began to give me signals that I should stop. Because of his signals my situation became even more difficult.

Restraining my laughing was so difficult for me, that I started biting on my lip to prevent bursting out laughing again. We were sitting like this for a quarter of an hour while suffering from our restrained giggles, before the break came and we finally could go bursting out laughing outside the classroom. In the meanwhile I had bitten through my lip until it had started bleeding. This emotion of restrained giggles in my case is so extremely strong, that it's preventing me to experience any trauma whatsoever. When you're losing control over your emotions, you're pulling at the red bolt of your trauma-catapult.

➤ To be able to experience trauma-meditation successfully, you ought to have a thorough command of two essential matters.

The first: You have to be able to bring yourself

into a light sleep, like it's explained in the take-off procedure. The sleep has to be deep enough to be able to evoke your trauma's from your subconsciousness. However, at this you should be aware not to lose your consciousness. You'll have to be able to keep thinking rationally. This is a matter of exercise.

The second matter is to take distance from your nasty emotions. You'll have to be able to separate yourself from your nasty emotions in a proper way and what's more, while doing so you'll have to keep thinking rationally. You'll have to carry out both these essential matters in a correct manner, before you're going to experience a trauma-meditation.

➢ The emotional condition of your flight-instructor has always to stay neutral, independent and impartial. But how are you going to manage this?
While disconnecting yourself from your nasty emotions it's important not to feel sorry for yourself. Otherwise you'll be carried away by your nasty emotions. As a result of this you're going to get stuck in the process of trauma-meditation. Have compassion with your apprentice instead of feeling sorry for him/her!

➢ A trauma-programming is a creative process. As soon as you get an image of a trauma, you shouldn't push it away. Experience your trauma once again. Pay attention to emotions which are evoked by this particular trauma. What are these emotions? Ask yourself. What does the apprentice need right now? Frequently you'll be able to feel this intuitively. Don't you know that? Imagine a similar situation, which you could encounter on the street. What would your reaction be, if you should see a mother treating her child with verbal violence? This is your answer. Is the apprentice already mature enough to handle this? Ask him what he needs at this very moment. That could be an action, an object or something else from your side as a flight instructor. Bring it into action. Sense what it does to the emotions of your apprentice. Does it help? Does it lessen the strength of his emotions? Go on. If it doesn't work, you should consider doing something else. See to it, that your action evokes a (positive) strong emotion on the side of the apprentice. The positive emotion has to be stronger than the nasty emotion. Sometimes it helps to demolish the nasty emotion as a brick wall step by step. That way you're creating a sequence of actions on the spot, which eventually is going to lead to the disappearing of the nasty emotions. You should to do this in the trial-and-error way. This is a way to find a solution.

I'm convinced that every child, who's younger than ten years, is being able to design this creative process. Consider a child who's coming home from the primary school (or childcare) in a totally upset state of mind, because something nasty happened between him/her and his/her classmates. He/she is emotional and he/she wants to get rid of his/her nasty emotions. How is he/she going to manage this? In his/her imagination he/she is going to create situations, in which he/she will be able to get rid of his/her nasty emotions. Or he/she is going to play out his/her nasty emotions in a game. This has been preprogrammed in our nature.

➢ During the trauma-meditation, traumas can enter your mind, which could be evoking such nasty emotions, that you're being overwhelmed and that you're losing control of your nasty emotions. In that case you're not going to manage to disconnect your nasty emotions from yourself. If that's the case: use the trauma-catapult.

➢ Do you sense fear for the unknown? Are you not sure that you could be able to tackle a forgotten trauma, which is emerging from your subconsciousness? If so, you're advised to keep an object in your arms, which gives you a feeling of safety during your trauma-meditation. This could be a stuffed toy to hug with or something similar. Or you could consider holding an object of a beloved one or a family member, who always cares (cared) about you.

The most important thing is that you'll be feeling secure in that situation.

➤ After a couple of trauma-meditations, the iceberg of nasty recollections is going to melt. Constantly new recollections and/or emotions will emerge. You don't know beforehand what you're going to encounter. Just let those new emotions come over you, experience them in your mind. Don't push them away. Nasty recollections and emotions can be healed during the trauma-mediation.

➤ Keep a logbook. Write down every experience in your trauma-meditation. Writing has a healing effect.

➤ How often can you perform the trauma-meditations? This depends on a number of factors. After my trauma-meditation with "kerosene" I have been sick for a couple of weeks. During that period I wasn't able to perform a single trauma-meditation. In case of other trauma-meditations, my traumas were not that radical (heavy) and that's why I was able to perform even two to three trauma-meditations a week. My advice: Don't go too fast! You can't operate all organs in your body at the same time. During every trauma-meditation you're opening a wound in your psyche. You treat the wound and you stick a plaster over it. After that you let nature do it's curing work. In due time the wound will be going to heal. So take sufficient time to let this healing process take place successfully. Take a long break before starting your next trauma-meditation. Start your sessions with a maximum of one trauma-meditation a week.

Uses of the trauma-meditation

The trauma-meditation can be successfully employed for the benefit of healing nasty emotions and Philippe-reactions as well as for the benefit of relieving an experience of physical feelings, such as pain.

Nasty emotions

- ☑ Fear of failure

- ☑ Fear of speaking in public

- ☑ Other fears

- ☑ Feeling of guilt

- ☑ Distress

- ☑ Disgust

- ☑ Impatience

- ☑ Despair

- ☑ Envy

- ☑ Hate

- ☑ Jealousy

- ☑ Shame

- ☑ Blame

- ☑ Despair

- ☑ Rage (Anger)

- ☑ Fear

- ☑ Anxiety

- ☑ Terror

- ☑ Anguish

- ☑ Scare

- ☑ Sadness

- ☑ Sorrow

- ☑ Grief

- ☑ Affliction

- ☑ Mourning

Philippe-reactions (reaction-patterns, behaviour and attitude)

- ☑ You can't stand criticism. You're quickly retreating into the defense.

- ☑ You rapidly feel being attacked.

- ☑ You're reacting exaggeratedly emotional on

some situations, people or pronunciations.

☑ You're feeling annoyed at some people or their behaviour.

☑ You don't like someone, without knowing the reason.

☑ You're a control-freak. You're avoiding mistakes.

☑ You're feeling exaggeratedly responsible for the other person.

☑ It's difficult for you to let go of certain things. You keep stuck to them and you keep worrying about them.

☑ You're feeling very vulnerable in certain situations without a clear reason.

☑ You're feeling unsafe in certain situations without an explainable reason.

☑ You're lacking selfconfidence.

☑ You're feeling insecure in certain situations.

☑ You're getting stressed in particular situations.

Physical feelings

What's happening to people when they're undergoing pain? They're suffering. Experiencing pain consists of two parts, namely a physical feeling of the pain and an emotional experience of the pain. The last mentioned experience makes the suffering worse. Caused by the trauma-meditation, emotional experience can be changed. An example. I always got scared when I was getting sick in the stomach. My fear used to make my experience of the sickness in the stomach quite a lot worse than it really was. Caused by the fear, my muscles began to get tense as a result of which my sickness in the stomach even kept on getting worse. Behind my fear was a sequence of traumas, which I treated successfully during the trauma-meditations. Thanks to these, I was able to disconnect my sickness of the stomach from the fear. Now I can simply be sick in the stomach without sensing fear. The sickness in the stomach is annoying, but I don't suffer that much from it any more.

You're not going to be able to relieve the physical pain by means of the trauma-meditation. But you surely can relieve the emotional experience (for instance the mental suffering).

Examples of physical feelings:

☑ Pain

☑ Nausea

☑ Tiredness

Physical feelings, nasty emotions and emotions which are evoked by the Philippe-reactions, can serve as a target-feeling during the trauma-meditation.

Let's pick a theme (subject) for the trauma-meditation. The most occurring problem among people consists of financial worries.

Relieve financial worries

Let's explore what the term "financial worries" means. Financial worries consist of a financial problem and the emotional handling of this problem. Your financial problem is a fact. Your emotional experience is your reaction on this fact. In the next pages I'm going to explain how you could manage to reduce your financial worries.

A financial problem

A financial problem itself is causing only a part of your financial worries. It's very important for your mind to make this fact as comprehensible and clear as possible.

Take the following steps:

Step 1. Make your financial situation comprehensible. It has to become a painting for your mind. What are your monthly earnings? What are your monthly spendings? How much money is left at the end of the month? Or how much is your financial deficit at the end of the month? To get an exact answer to this questions, you can obtain a simple budget planner through our website. You can find the name of this website in the Epilogue of this book.

Step 2. What exactly is the problem? What is the worst thing that could happen? Most likely there will be different scenario's.

Step 3. Make an action plan for each scenario. Which steps can you take to get out of your money shortage? It's very important to put every scenario in writing. Now make a drawing of each scenario. For instance: because of financial problems you'll have to sell your beloved car. Now the most important moment has arised. Ask yourself: what am I feeling right now? Which emotions does this evoke in me? Those are the bad (nasty) emotions which are responsible for your worries. Make a note of these bad emotions. You're going to need them soon for your trauma-meditation.

Emotional experience

From my own experience I dare say, that in fact a financial problem happens to be less heavy as it's being experienced emotionally. Our nasty emotions are making the problem that heavy and gloomy. If you get to the roots of those nasty emotions, you're going to be confronted with your fears. A fear to lose, a fear to fail, a fear concerning the decreased well-being of your beloved one(s), etc. Finally you're going to realize that, no matter how serious your financial problems may be, you're not going to die from it. You've made your action plan for each scenario. You know what you have to do or what you can do. So what 's the use to keep on brooding and worrying that much? From my own experience I know that my worries are coming from two sources. These sources are my nasty emotions from the past and my uncertainty about the future. My uncertainty about the future is being fed by my nasty emotions. My uncertainty is just like an oil well, which has been set on fire. This well is going to keep on burning as long as there's still oil left inside it. That burning oil represents my nasty emotions from the past, which are looking for their way out. Or to put it in a nutshell: the fire of my uncertainty keeps burning as long as the oil of my nasty emotions is present in the well of my past.

With the aid of the trauma-meditation you'll be able to expel your nasty emotions. This is going to relieve your worries. To clarify this, I selected a few samples:

December 15

I'm just back from Jennifer, my psychologist. She told me that the coverage of the basic package of the health care insurance is going to change from January 1st. This means that I'll have to pay a yearly personal contribution to the amount of € 200,- for her services. Next to the legal amount of one's own risk (being € 220,-) , the total amount is going to increase to € 420,-- a year. This is almost half of my monthly allowance. That's a lot of money for me. I'm worrying a lot about this. I don't know yet if I'll be able to yield this huge amount.

I'm at home now. When I'm trying to cope with my financial worries, I'm sensing an enormous feeling of distress.

Target-feeling

The feeling of distress. It's being stucked in my throat. I'm concentrating on this feeling.

Image

I'm seeing a little Filipp, not more than five years old. He's upset and he's crying. His mother is furious. She gives an enormous smack on his head, as a result of which he's going to scream even louder. He's totally shaken and in a state of shock.

I interfere. I wrap up the mother with wrapping plastic and I attach her to the wall. She's in a vacuum and she's not being able to do anything at all anymore. I make a hole in the plastic near her mouth and her nose to make it possible for her to be able to breath. Her anger doesn't allow itself to calm down.

I take little Filipp into my arms and I give him my love. He's crying and he's calling for Baba (grandmother) I keep holding him in my arms for a short while. Afterwards we're going to our trauma-paradise. Grandma receives him with loving care.

I'm looking around. Tens and tens of little Filipp's of different ages are playing in and around the water. I go to them. All of them are running towards me. They are very happy to see me. Like little monkeys they're clinging to my arms, shoulders, neck and legs. They're dragging me into the water. And then the big game begins! Clouds caused by the spattered water are hanging around me. We're having a lot of fun among each other. They're all happy and they want to go on with this endlessly. I realize that I should give them more attention in my daily life. Little Filipp, whom I took to his grandma, doesn't want to let loose of her. He's sitting on her knee and he grabs her dress with both his little hands, but his attention has totally been absorbed by the playing in the water. He would rather start running to that spot right away, but the feeling of safety that he has, while being with his grandma, still prevents him from going. I'm standing in the middle of the water- game. It didn't last very long anymore before he lets go of her. He's running towards me, puts his arms around my leg and he starts joining the game with one little hand. It's all right now. I'm feeling it!

Back to the target-feeling

It's true that the feeling of distress is still there, but it definitely has decreased. I'm concentrating on this.

Image

I'm seeing Filipp, being between thirteen and fifteen years old. There is a row going on in the house. His mother is angry. He wants to stand up for himself. This attitude only makes her more angry. Finally she says: "You get the hell out of my house! You're not my son anymore!" Filipp is being expelled from the house. It's late, dark and cold (it's the end of December). He has nowhere to go. He's going to the apartment building across the street and he's going to sit down on a concrete step in the stairwell. It's very cold inside. The stairwell isn't being heated. Quite a long time ago the heating system had burst and hasn't been repaired ever since. You can see a pack of ice lying on the radiators. It's very dark in there. He feels the coldness of the concrete staircase step. He's very distressed and he senses that nasty feeling in his throat.

I'm going to interfere. I try to embrace him. He immediately refuses this. H's too big (old) for that! I'm going to sit beside him on the stairs. I can't do anything at all. I'm just listening. Suddenly he starts to talk. "I don't understand why she's hating me that much. Why? I'm doing my utmost, but without any result whatsoever. I have nobody except her. Why did I end up in this situation and in this loveless life? What did I do wrong? I don't get it at all. Why? Please tell me why, for heavens sake! (I feel a whole lot of sorrow and mental pain coming up). He starts crying. I try to embrace him, but it doesn't succeed that well. Suddenly I'm seeing Yvon (my current girlfriend). She's embracing him and she gives him a kiss on his forehead. She keeps her lips touching his forehead and she's giving him a lot of loving care. On the inside Filipp is completely run-down. He has totally run out of energy and he's entirely empty. I try to encourage him and to give him some of my energy. I'm telling him that his mother and this situation are only temporary and that he should try to survive this period. Eventually his emotions are going to calm down. He's accepting the situation as it is. It feels the same as if your beloved one has died and you now have accepted it at last. We take him home and say farewell. It's about two o'clock in the morning. He rings at the door. His mother opens the door and she's looking at him disapprovingly. In her look I see that she's wondering if Filipp is at last mentally broken or not (yet). Because THAT'S what she wants from the bottom of "her heart".

Filipp is allowed to go to bed right away...

Post-control of my target-feeling

It's all right now. I don't feel any sorrow anymore. But I feel that I still need time to let this wound heal. From now on nature is going to take it over from me.

All of a sudden I'm able to let go my financial worries. "We'll see", I say to myself. About that matter I'm having a quiet feeling now.

January 30

I just heard on the news, that the rates of the Dutch dentists are unlimited as of January 1. This means that their rates are not legally limited anymore and that they are allowed to determine their tariffs themselves. In Rotterdam a dentist is charging € 140,- for filling up a cavity. This is three times more than the legally decided standard tariff which was applied before January 1. I'm feeling uncertainty about the future. If I should get a toothache and consequently should need a root canal treatment, I wonder how I'm going to pay for that. I'm worrying a lot about this. When I'm concentrating on my way of sensing, I feel sorrow accumulating (piling up) in my throat. If I'm directing my attention at this spot, I'm sensing a tight and panicky feeling.

Target-feeling

The feeling in my throat. I'm concentrating on that.

Image

I'm seeing myself. I'm not more than five years old and I'm lost in a forest, somewhere in Siberia. It's common knowledge, that the forests in Siberia are so vast, that you can travel through them for hundreds of kilometres without meeting a single soul. Getting lost in such a forest could mean your death. I'm seeing nobody. I don't know what to do. I'm panicking and I'm sensing an enormous tension. I interfere. I take little Filipp in my arms and I give him my love. He's beginning to feel safe and he's getting quiet. I take him to his mother. She's not aware of what happened to little Filipp. She's sitting at the table talking rubbish with other people. Little Filipp is feeling safe now.

Back to the target-feeling

Image

I'm seeing little Filipp, being no more than five years old. He's alone on the street. He doesn't know where his mother is. He's in panic, feeling tense and he's on the verge of bursting into tears. I take him in my arms and I give him my love. He's becoming quiet and he's relaxing. I take him to his mother.

Back to the target-feeling

Image

I'm seeing little Filipp. He's very sad, upset and he's crying. His mother says that he should not cry. Fortunately she's not angry and not aggressive. Eventually she's taking him in her arms and little Filipp is getting quiet.

Back to the target-feeling

Image

I'm seeing little Filipp. He's being beaten on his head by his mother. It hurts a lot (I can exactly feel the spot on the top of my head where she has hit him). She's aggressive and she's yelling at him very hard. She's abusing, disparaging and intimidating him. She also says that he's irritating her nerves tremendously and that she would gladly kill him. Even if that means that she should be imprisoned thereafter, she wouldn't feel sorry for her deed. I interfere. I fasten her hand with a handcuff to a door-handle of our cupboard. She's so mad about this that she jerks off the door of the build-in cupboard. I fasten her with a pair of handcuffs to the wall. She doesn't want to calm down. She looks like a wild tiger who has just been captured. She's boiling with rage. I take little Filipp in my arms and I give him a lot of loving care. His head hurts. He doesn't feel safe because his mother is so very much infuriated. I grab a big spray can filled with shaving foam. With this can I'm going to spray the mother all over. We can only see her nose between the white foam. This way she's still being able to breath. I take little Filipp with me to the trauma-paradise, where he's being taken care of by his grandma. She gives him a lot of loving care. He's feeling okay now.

Back to the target-feeling

Image

Little Filipp is playing in the sea. Suddenly a big wave is coming ashore. Little Filipp is struck by panic and almost drowns. He gets water in his nose and in his throat. He nearly chokes. He's coughing. I take him in my arms. He keeps coughing. A lot of seawater is coming out of his mouth. Gradually he's becoming quiet. I give him a fruit juice. He's drinking eagerly. I take him with me to our trauma-paradise. He's very glad to see his grandma again.

Back to the target-feeling

Image

Little Philipp has a hiccup. It's quite awful. His entire body is tightening. It won't wear off. I take him in my arms and give him love. He's relaxing. Gradually it's wearing off. Afterwards I take him with me to our trauma-paradise.

Post-control of my target-feeling

My target-feeling has disappeared.

Step 6. Forgiving and letting go

From my own experience I can say that there are two kinds of "wrongdoers" in my trauma's. The wrongdoers are people who did something to me in the past. The first kind is a stranger. It's a person with whom I didn't had an emotional link. For example a boy from my school who was pestering me and who wasn't a friend of mine. The second kind is a person with whom I did rather had an emotional link. For example my mother, whom I love or a close friend whom I used to trust. So the emotional link is the love for my mother and the trust in my friend.

So with type two I had an emotional link before the trauma. This emotional link has made the nasty emotions even more intense and worse. That's why this emotional link has caused the coping with the trauma to be so difficult. So for the benefit of type two I had to add an additional step to my trauma healing. This step is called "forgiving". How should you do this? I wondered. How do you forgive someone? Forgiving is a process. I'm going to explain this process to you.

I couldn't forgive my mother because I was mad at her. Why was I mad? I had two reasons for being mad at her. The first reason are my trauma's, which were causing a continuous supply of nasty emotions. The second reason is my thought: "Why did she act this way, as a result of which these trauma's arised!? I don't

217

understand her behaviour". As this thought is constantly being nourished by my nasty emotions, I keep turning around in a vicious circle (nasty emotions - thought - nasty emotions - thought - etc.). I try to understand her and consequently this again evokes these nasty emotions. These emotions are intensifying my thoughts. I can't let it go. My thoughts are again evoking the nasty emotions and as a result of this the process starts all over again. I look like a running mouse in a tredmill. How can I break through this vicious circle? Initially I had to close off the nourishment of my thoughts. When my nasty emotions cannot nourish my thoughts anymore, I eventually am able to think rationally. I removed these nasty emotions by means of my trauma-meditations. Now only the answer to the "why"-question still remains open. I want to understand the behaviour of my mother. Without having understood that behaviour, I'll not be able to accept the things she did to me. So I'll have to find the answer to my "why-question". As soon as I know why she did it, I might be able to forgive her. After having forgiven her, I'll be able to let it go. Letting it go means that the nasty events, which have been dominating my life, can be stored in my memory as being "processed" (fixed or healed). A life-event has been "processed" when all nasty emotions and negative thoughts about this event have been finally erased from the memory.

Steps in the process of forgiving and letting go

Step 1. Healing of nasty emotions. Getting rid of your nasty emotions to be able to think rationally, without being carried away by your emotions.

Step 2. Understanding the reason. Learning to understand the cause why he or she did that to you.

Step 3. Accepting

Step 4. Forgiving and letting go.

To enable you to understand this process better, I'll lead you through my own process of "forgiving and letting go".

Step 1 Healing of nasty emotions

I described this step in my trauma-meditations. See my logbook of trauma-meditations. The purpose of this step is to get rid of my nasty emotions. I handled a stack of traumas, in which my mother was the wrongdoer. After having made this step I was able to think rationally, without being carried away by my nasty emotions. Nasty emotions are standing in the way of rational thinking, so also on the path which leads to understanding the reason(s) behind the behaviour of my mother.

Step 2 Understanding the reason

To give you a clear view of the method of working of this step I'm first going to tell you my history in short.

My place of birth

I was born in the southern part of European-Russia, in a city called Astrakhan. This city, originally a Mongolian khanat, on the year 1333 was part of the Golden Horde khanat, which was founded bij the grandson of the well-known Mongolian conqueror Dzjengis Khan. Nomad's, Western Mongol's (Kalmyk's) brought the Tibetan Buddhism to the region. In 1771 the Russian Empress Catherina the Great transformed the Kalmyken khanat into a Russian province. Despite the monopoly of the Russian Orthodox Church, the Buddhism was counted among the so-called "tolerant "religions. After the Russian revolution in 1917 the communist party came to power, which led to exterminate the Buddhism in the region. Ordered by Joseph Stalin, in 1931 a collectivistic state system was installed. The Buddhist monasteries were closed, the religious texts were burned and all monks were deported to the working camps in Siberia. There they awaited the same fate as the Tibetan monks went through in the working camps of communistic China.

After the collapse of the Soviet Union in 1991, Buddhism revived in the independent republic of Kalmykia.

In the capital of Kalmykia, Elista, the largest Buddhist temple of Europe was built. The Golden temple, a worldwide Buddhist study-centre, with a nine metres high Buddha statue, which was opened in 2005 by the Dalai Lama. Apart from a lot of other well-known people, among others, the temple has been visited by Hollywood-star and Buddhist Steven Seagal. Kalmykia, inhabited by almost three hundred thousand people, is the only Buddhist region in Europe.

My parents

My grandmother Katja always used to fancy southern male types. In 1937 she was going to marry a city-architect, who was Greek by birth. A few days before their wedding, he was arrested by the former KGB and sentenced to "enemy of the people and the communist party" and he was deported to the working camps in Siberia. He never came back. Just like millions of other people, he fell as a victim of Stalin's repression campaign, as a result of which the country had to be "purified" of (possible) political opponents. The chief of the department of the local authority, where my grandmother was working as a budget inspector, had also been arrested and tortured. Katja had to come to the KGB to be interrogated and there she saw her chief with a swollen bloody face, broken arms and bloody wounds. She was forced to sign a forged statement. Otherwise the same fate as that of her chief and her Greek lover, awaited her.

Just before the second world war she meets a new love, a surgeon, with whom in 1940 in Leningrad (Saint Petersburg) she gets a daughter, called Violette, my mother. In 1941 the second world war breaks out. My mother's father leaves to the enemy front as an officer of the medical service. My mother, a one year old child, is being exposed to the horrors of war. Starvation, suffering, bombardments and death people (all around) are causing a considerable deep imprint (impact) in her subconsciousness. Her father is writing love letters to his wife Katja. However he's not coming back home. During the war at the frontline, he's getting a relationship with a woman-colleague, with whom he's going to share his life from that time on. After the war my grandmother, Katja, is going to divorce from her husband (my grandfather). Katja becomes a single mother. Violette is suddenly going to suffer from health problems in her adolescence. Without any distinct cause she quits eating and as a consequence she's getting a grave underweight. Her doctors are not being able to explain this development. Everything possible is being tried out and done to get her eating again. It will take another couple of years before she'll be back on her former weight.

Violette, almost eighteen years old now, is going to visit her father on his request. After having been traveling by train for two days, she arrives at the station early in the morning. He's not there. After a while she sees him coming with his new wife and her sister. "What are you doing here?", his wife asks. "I have come to visit my father", answers Violette. "YOU HAVE GOT NO FATHER!", she says. Her father turns back and he leaves with his giggling women, who evidently are having him under their thumb. The reluctant witnesses are speechless. Nobody dares to say something. Silence. They'll see to it that Violette will be getting home safely. Her life is going on. She's going to study. She had a way of making herself the center of attention on the university continuously. Anywhere she wants to be the first one, the best one and the smartest one. After her academical study she meets a man, my father, whom she's going to marry. They don't manage to fulfill their wish to have children. My mother cannot get pregnant. After five years of undergoing numerous painful treatments, she's being told that there is no hope anymore. Accepting this fact lies a heavy burden on the relationship with her husband. Their life goes on. Unexpected by everyone my mother gets pregnant anyway. Unfortunately her happiness is rapidly spoiled by a discovery. Her husband is cheating her with his secretary, who is already pregnant from him. The situation is hopeless. Two pregnant women with one man. My mother decides to make a final decision. She packs her bags and she leaves for Astrakhan. A few months later she's having me after a heavy delivery. Violette is becoming a single mother.

As a five years old child, I'm telling my mother my little secret in complete confidence. I did a pee in my trousers. It was a little accident which I had kept hidden for others and of which I was very ashamed. "Men of five years old don't pee in their trousers", I said to my mother. My mother has sworn to me not to tell this to anybody whatsoever. At the next party at our home, she told at the dinner table to her twelve guests all about my remark and little accident. Everybody thought it to be very funny and they laughed in full. Everyone looked at me. I felt being made ridiculous. She had betrayed me. I felt sorrow and a lot of shame. I was sitting at the end of the table and I wondered how she could do something like that to me! If I couldn't trust my own mother, who's left to be trusted anyway? This wasn't a once-only incident. This resulted in the fact, that I began hiding my feelings. I'm ten years old. My grandmother dies and this has an enormous impact on my mother. The anger of my mother is becoming more furious. She's getting tremendous outbursts of rage, during which she's often totally blowing her top. She's ruthless. I'm afraid that one of these days she might finish me off. I'm constantly living under stress.

What's the matter with my mother?

According to my psychologist Jennifer, my mother is suffering from severe personality disorders from the so-called B-cluster. In psychology cluster B is being called the dramatic, emotional, impulsive cluster. This cluster consists of four personality disorders: Borderline, Antisocial, Narcissistic and Histrionic personality disorder. After having examined these disorders, I came to the conclusion that my mother is suffering from all of these disorders. In other words, my mother is mentally ill to a grave extent. This is the reason of her behaviour. I wondered what could be the origin of her illness. The answer to this is quite simple. The illness already became its first roots in 1941, the second year of my mother's life, when her at that specific age not yet fully developed psyche, was being exposed to the horrors of the second world war. What's happening to a child when it hears an explosion of a bomb? Isn't that like undergoing the same psycho-physiological trauma-tizing process as Little Albert experienced when he heard the loud sound? I think it is.

Trauma-dominoes- effect

Traumatized people are producing (giving birth to) traumatized children. One generation is passing on its trauma's to the next generation.

My grandmother with her husband in 1940

My mother (1 year old) with my grandmother in 1941

My mother (8 years old) in 1948

My grandmother with my mother in 1948

My father at the age of 26

Wedding of my parents in 1965

My mother at the age of 67 in 2007

I always wondered how my life would have been if my grandmother could have been married to her Greek lover, my mother hadn't been forced to go through a war and the father of my mother hadn't been sent to the enemy front. In fact two people have determined the fate of my ancestors, like they did in the case of millions of other people. These people were Stalin and Hitler. Millions of human beings have been killed and the ones who survived their dictatorships, are traumatized. How do you become such a person like Stalin or like Hitler?

Stalin

The family where Josef Stalin was born in 1879, was living under poor circumstances. Caused by the poverty in the family, Josef was the only one of the four children who survived. He himself almost died of small pox at the age of five. Stalin's father was an alcoholic, who had a thorough command of the language of violence. Josef has often been gravely beaten and maltreated by his father.

In 1907, after merely one year of marriage, Stalin's first wife, Jekaterina Svanidze, dies. After the funeral, Stalin says: "This creature knew how to soften my heart of stone. But she died and with her my last warm feelings for mankind also died". Jekaterina leaves him a son, called Jacob. The hard and cruel way in which Stalin is treating his son, results in an attempted suicide by the latter. Jacob tried to shot himself in 1928, but he survived the attempt. Stalin reacts: "He can't even shoot properly!".

In 1927, the Russian neurologist and psychiatrist Vladimir Bechterev, well-known on account of the Bechterev disease, determines the diagnosis "far advanced persecution insanity complex" in case of Stalin and he consequently recommends immediate retirement. After some time Bechterev suddenly and very unexpected dies.

Hitler

The father of Adolf Hitler was born as an illegitimate son. Like Stalin this father also used to maltreat his son Adolf and his other children. For that reason the eldest brother fled from home for good at the age of thirteen years old. This way the seven years old Adolf found himself in the middle of the violent attention of his aggressive and authoritarian father. In 1903 his father suddenly died, leaving the thirteen years old Adolf behind as head of the family. When he got older, just like his father, Adolf also got outbursts of anger. In 1907 Adolf's mother, whom he loved very much, dies from breast cancer. Her suffering and her final death has a great impact on the eighteen years old Adolf. He develops a phobia about illnesses. Like Stalin, Hitler doesn't manage to escape from his persecution insanity complex.

My mother, Stalin and Hitler did not have any form of safety during their youth. Also each one of them has lost a beloved one, which just intensified their trauma's. Please don't get me wrong, it's absolutely not my intention to justify the crimes and atrocities of Stalin and Hitler. They shall remain fully responsible for their deeds for once and for all. I'm merely looking for the tiny spot in the course of history, where the seeds of my own traumas have been planted. I now understand that the youth-traumas, like those of my mother, are causing a chain reaction. I have got my traumas owing to my mother's behaviour. She herself has been traumatized among other things by people who also had been traumatized during their youth. I define this as a trauma-dominoes-effect or a trauma-chain-reaction, which already has been wandering about the world for ages. Besides individual people, there are also whole nations which are haunted by war-trauma's. For instance think about Jews or other nations. The second world war has not been the first and certainly will not be the last (global) war on our planet. At one place or another there's always a war going on, which is liable to cause a new chain-reaction-trauma.

Step 3 Acceptation

I now understand the background reasons of my mother's deed's. She herself is a victim of her time. I don't want to blame her for everything she did to me, but on the other hand I don't want to discharge her from the responsibility for her deed's. It's like it is. I'm at peace with this now.

Step 4 To forgive and let go

Now is the moment that I'm able to let go of my youth-trauma's. This doesn't bother me because my nasty emotions have been healed and I've understood the reason of my mother's behaviour. Now my youth is merely a chapter out of a book about my own history. I have forgiven my mother.

A license for parents

How can the trauma-chain-reaction be stopped? A trauma in a psyche of a child cannot always be visible at first sight. The consequences of such a trauma can usually not reveal itself until the child has reached the age of an adult. Of course far from everybody has had a traumatic youth. But is everyone capable of being a good parent? Can everyone give sufficient love, affection, safety, care and a suitable upbringing to a child of his/her own? Does everyone have sufficient insight into him/herself? The answer is no. In my opinion future parents should volunteer to undergo a psychological test before they decide to actually fulfill their wish to have a child. Passed? In that case you'll get a license of appropriateness. A kind of driver's license for parents so to speak. Failed? First you should work on yourself, seek help and try again after a few years. In fact this already happens in case of people who want to adopt a child. They have to go through a great many tests and procedures, because the responsible authorities want to be sure that they dispose of the necessary skills to be able to function as good parents.

Why are these people, who for biological reasons can't have a child of their own, being extensively tested for their future parenting, while the others merely have to go to bed with each other to bring a child into the world? Where lies the boundary of justice in this matter? Would my mother have been able to get a "parental license"? The answer is no. I, as her son, would rather have been born with a mother who gives love instead of (verbal) violence. Traumatized people are costing the community millions of euro's. Consider (think of) allowances, health-care-costs, damages to third parties, etc. Therefore the possession of the parental "parental license" doesn't only mean taking responsibility for the benefit of your own child, but eventually also for the consequences which have to be paid for by the community in the future. I qualify this as being a conscious reproduction of mankind. In many countries there are institutions which take care of child welfare, but nowhere there is something similar like for instance birth protection. When a child has been born and is living in a traumatized environment, in fact it's already too late to take adequate measures. In the Netherlands children from families with a traumatized environment are being removed from their homes by a Bureau Youth Care. The child who is being removed from its natural living environment and is being separated from its parents, is in fact already going through a traumatic experience. That's the reason why a parental "parental license" could serve as a proper birth protection measure.

Working section

It's time to start working. How well are you settled in your own emotional world? Are you always well aware of your emotions, which are hiding themselves behind your reactions? How many Philippe-reactions and nasty emotions can you mention now? Write them down in your diary of target-feelings. You can let the nasty emotions be dealt with in your trauma-meditation.

Diary of target-feelings

Make a note of your Philippe-reactions and/or your nasty emotions.

1. ....

2. ....

3. ....

4. ....

5. ....

6. ....

7. ....

8. ....

9. ....

10. ....

To begin

The best you can do is to learn the technique of "Mindfulness based trauma treatment" in steps. Just like learning to drive a car, you shouldn't immediately start stepping on the gas. Start with the basis of meditating and mindfulness. Make sure that you have been sufficiently sunk into the depth of your meditation without losing your consciousness (falling asleep). Practice a couple of times to distance yourself from your nasty emotion(s). As soon as you are ready, then first you should try to practice the trauma-meditation without the trauma-hunting. You can use this kind of trauma-meditation for your nasty memories, of which you yourself are well aware. You don't need to go searching for them in your subconsciousness. These are nasty experiences from your past, which you commonly remember and which you can effortless evoke in your mind. In the trauma-meditation without trauma-hunting, the trauma-hunting step is being skipped. After your take-off procedure, you should immediately begin with trauma-programming.

If this trauma-meditation has been successful, you can start the trauma-meditation including trauma-hunting.

Procedure of trauma-meditation without trauma-hunting

This procedure is meant for nasty experiences from your past, of which you are already (or still) aware. You can concsiously evoke a recollection. For example: I'm thinking of a specific experience from my past. The image immediately penetrates my mind and evokes nasty emotions inside me.

Take-off procedure

Sit down nicely. Close your eyes and relax your mind. Concentrate yourself on your breathing in a relaxed way. Follow your breathing attentively. Let your thoughts flow away. Let your mind fall into a light sleep, but don't lose your consciousness.

Trauma-programming

Now evoke a self-chosen nasty recollection (image, movie), which calls up a nasty emotion in your mind. Experience this recollection. Ask yourself: "Which nasty emotion does this traumatic experience evoke in me?". Take distance from this emotion. Look at the image in a rational way. Make contact, if possible, with your trainee. What does he need now? Ask yourself what this nasty emotion is evoking in him. Is that a situation of an action of someone? How can I change that situation, so the trainee can utter his nasty emotion in the image? What actions can I create, so the trainee is coming out of the traumatic experience with positive emotions? Keep constantly watching the emotional state of the trainee. At the end, take the trainee to your trauma-paradise.

Target-feeling check

If all went well, your target-feeling has become less strong now. Ask yourself the question: How strong is the target-feeling right now? Concentrate yourself again on your target-feeling. Repeat the steps of trauma-hunting and trauma-programming until your target-feeling is getting beneath 10 percent of the original strength.

Logbook of your trauma-meditation's

Make a note of your trauma-meditations in your logbook. Watch your emotional state while writing. What's changed in your emotional experience of your trauma's? It could well be that while you're writing new emotions or memories are entering your mind. Make a mote of this in your diary of target-feelings.

Procedure trauma-meditation with trauma-hunting

This procedure is meant for the nasty experiences, which you have "forgotten". You're suffering from nasty emotions. You don't know which nasty experiences are responsible for that. For example. I'm feeling a lot of unrest, but I haven't the faintest idea where it's coming from.

Take-off procedure

Sit down comfortably. Close your eyes and relax your mind. Concentrate yourself on your breathing in a relaxed way. Follow (the rhythm of) your breathing with attention. Let your thoughts flow away. Let your mind fall into the light sleep, but don't lose your consciousness.

Trauma-hunting

Now call up a recent experience, which evokes a nasty emotion in your mind. Dissociate yourself from this nasty emotion and let the experience flow away out of your mind. Now this nasty emotion is your target-feeling. Determine the place of the target-feeling in your body (your throat, your breast, etc.). Direct your attention to this place. Now concentrate yourself on the target-feeling and wait. Don't have expectations. Just keep sitting with your attention focused on your target-feeling and wait until an image (recollection) is coming to your mind.

Trauma-programming

Now you should have a nasty recollection (image, movie). Experience this recollection. Ask yourself the question which nasty emotion evokes this traumatic experience in your mind. Distance yourself from this emotion. Look at the image in a rational way. If it's possible, get in touch with your trainee. What does he need right now? Ask yourself: What is this nasty emotion evoking in him? Is it a situation or an action of somebody? How can I change this situation or action, as a result of which the trainee can express his nasty emotion in the image? What can I bring into action, as a result of which the trainee will be coming out of the traumatic experience with a positive emotion? You should constantly watch the emotional state of the trainee. Take the trainee at the end of the session to your trauma-paradise.

Target-feeling check

If all went well, your target-feeling has become less strong now. Ask yourself how strong its presence is right now. Concentrate yourself again on your target-feeling. Repeat the steps of trauma-hunting and trauma-programming until your target-feeling has reached a strength, which is lower than 10 percent of the original strength.

Logbook of your trauma-meditations

Make a note in your logbook of your trauma-meditation. Watch your emotional state during the time of your writing. What has been changed in the emotional experience of your trauma's? It might be possible that during the writing new emotions or memories are coming into your mind. Make a note of this possibility in your diary of target-feelings.

* Should there be no images (recollections) coming to your mind, this could mean that:

- ➤ You haven't sunk deep enough into the meditation (light sleep). That's why you have no access to your subconsciousness.

- ➤ Your head is full of thoughts. Your attention is wandering off from the target-feeling. Your thoughts are blocking the access to your subconsciousness.

- ➤ Your intention is ambiguous. You're imagining that you're eager to track down your nasty memories, whereas your feeling is telling you, that you rather don't feel like confronting yourself with your nasty memories.

- ➤ You're full of anticipation what's going to happen. Before you're going to hunt, you're expecting beforehand that you're going to shoot a duck with white feathers. For example: You expect that the target-feeling is going to evoke a certain memory in your mind.Consequently you're going to program the result of your trauma-hunting in your own mind. That's definitely not the intention. That way your expectations are blocking a free access to your subconsciousness.

➢ You're tense while concentrating on the target-feeling. Concentration means, that you should direct your attention on your target-feeling in a relaxed way.

➢ You have taken no (or insufficient) distance from your nasty emotions. By not doing so, you have let yourself being carried away. For instance: You're sensing so much (unconscious) anxiety, that you're blocking the access to your subconsciousness, because you don't dare to be confronted with the nasty memories from your past.

Logbook of trauma-meditations

Date

Situation

....
....
....
....
....
....
....
....

Target-feeling

....
....
....

Image (nasty memory and trauma-programming)

....
....
....
....
....
....
....
....
....

....
....
....
....
....
....
....
....
....
....
....
....
....
....
....
....
....
....
....
....
....
....
....
....
....
....
....
....
....
....
....
....
....

Metaphors

Where is my place in this life?

Metaphor "The Tiny Tin"

Once upon a time there was a very big supermarket, where a whole lot of articles were for sale.

One day a stockroom worker went to re-stock the shelves. He put tens and tens of different tiny tins on a cart and took them with him to the shopping department. On the way he lost one tiny tin. The following night the tiny tin wakes up, thinking: "Hey, I'm not lying in the right place! It's cold, dark and it doesn't feel good. I should be lying somewhere else!".

The tiny tin got up and went to find his place in the supermarket. He walked around the whole supermarket row after row and he couldn't find "his place" anywhere. The tiny tin felt unhappy and he kept on looking for his place, until he ran into a mouse. "Hello mouse", the tiny tin said, "Can you show me my place? ". "Sure I can", the mouse said. "You're round, you've got those little stripes with little numbers underneath at the side, I've seen little tins like you near the way out on the right side, I think you'll have to be there", the mouse said.

The tiny tin went to the indicated spot and he sat down between the other tiny tins. After having been there for one week, the tiny tin didn't feel happy at all. He didn't feel at home. The tiny tin only saw people with dogs walking past him, without showing any interest in him at all. The tiny tin asked another tiny tin, which was standing next to him: "Why am I feeling unhappy here?".

"This is not the right place for you", his neighbour said to him. "Is that so? Where should I be then?", the tiny tin asked. "I don't know for sure", the neighbour said. "As far as I'm concerned, I think you're looking very tough. If I were you, I would try to get a place at the soft drink section!".

The tiny tin went to the shelves, which are reserved for the soft drinks and he sat down there. After a week the tiny tin still felt unhappy and he went to ask a piece of advice from a tiny tin containing soft drink. The soft drink tiny tin happened to be an old, wise, over-dated tiny tin. "Soft drink" said: "If I were you, I would fetch me a new little label in the stockroom. You only have to know which label is the best for you to be sold at the best possible price. That's what every tiny tin wants, isn't it?" "Yes", the tiny tin said. "I would very much like to be sold at the best possible price!".

The tiny tin went to the stockroom to fetch a new label. In the stockroom they told him that it might last another two years until the new label would be ready and that the tiny tin should do his utmost to become someone who eventually is going to be mentioned on this new label.

The next night the tiny tin had a dream. In his dream THE BIG TIN-OPENER appeared and said to him: "I'm the truth, I'm the path of life of every tiny tin. Your content determines your place in the supermarket and definitely not the label you're wearing. Only in this way you can be fulfilled with the feeling of satisfaction and happiness".

Use your "self-opener" and you're going to find what you're looking for.

Living with a trauma

The little toilet roll

Like many of his other little brothers and sisters, the little toilet roll was born in a large factory. Shortly after his birth he had an accident. He fell into a bucket filled with water and he almost drowned. Somebody picked him out of the bucket and put him back on the shelf. It took a while before the little toilet roll was dried up again. After a couple of years the little toilet roll had managed to wipe this incident out of his memory. He lived the life of a happy little toilet roll, at least that was what he thought. Yet he regularly experienced a couple of nasty emotions, which could not be explained by a clear reason. He was afraid of buckets and water. Who cares, the little toilet roll thought, as long as I keep avoiding these two, there's nothing to worry about. All went quite well until the moment when he got a job in a ladies toilet of a fast food restaurant. He was disappointed of continuously having to get in touch with water and buckets. Obviously right from the start this was noticeable in his behaviour as well as in his employees attitude. It was not before long that his guests began to complain. The rumor spread that he was being rough towards his guests. During his first performance appraisal the little toilet roll was talked to about his roughness. "I haven't the slightest idea what I'm doing wrong", the little toilet roll responded. "You are rough! You should look at yourself in the mirror!". That's what his supervisor said. After this discussion the little toilet roll felt both frustrated and sad. He didn't know what to do. Finally he came to the conclusion that it wasn't his fault. The guests and his supervisor, who didn't have any idea of the qualitative good service he provided, were to blame instead. Life doesn't merely consist of working, he thought. He went to a party which was also being frequented by other little toilet rolls. Everybody was talking about the work they were involved in. "I personally", said a little pink toilet roll, "serve fifty guests a day!". "And I'm serving seventy", someone else shouted. "And I'm doing eighty", yet another little toilet roll called out "Hey," someone said. "Do you see that fat toilet roll over there? The one who is driving around in a BMW? Everybody knows him! He's working at a gas station. He's doing 250 customers a day! All his customers are satisfied. He doesn't bother about customer loyalty at all and yet he has hundreds of regular customers!" Due to this kind of conversations, the little toilet roll felt even more miserable. What could be the reason that other little toilet rolls seemed to be that successful in their career and he wasn't? He didn't get it at all. He asked for advice to another little toilet roll, who was wearing a coat covered with images of little funny dogs. Maybe you should show another attitude while serving a guest, was the advice of the other little toilet roll. The little toilet roll decided to follow his advice. He has tried out all the possible attitudes he could imagine. Nevertheless his clients kept complaining. At home he couldn't share his worries with his wife. Their discussions about his touchiness again and again resulted in a quarrel. He was convinced that it wasn't his fault. Every evening she was asking the very same question. How were things at your work today? Busy, I had a lot of heavy cases to solve, he used to answer briefly. This way it happened day in and day out. One day he saw another little toilet roll at his work place "Hey!? Who are you? This is my working area! Get lost!", shouted the little toilet roll. "You're looking into the mirror right now, I'm your reflection", the other little toilet roll said. "What do you mean? Reflection? What do you want from me?, called the little toilet roll, "You're continuously making appointments with others. You're constantly preoccupied with the problems of others. I'm also having problems and needs of my own. When are you ever going to make an appointment with me?", his reflection asked. "I haven't got the time for those things!", the little toilet roll shouted and he sprayed a thick layer of toilet freshener on the mirror, as a result of which his reflection wasn't visible anymore.

At his work things got increasingly worse. The guests (clients) kept complaining. Bad word-of-mouth advertising caused a reduction of the number of guests in the fast food restaurant. Even an insurance-claim for damage occurred! His guest, a middle-aged woman, had been damaged by the service of the little rough toilet roll. She claimed a full compensation of her medical expenses and a substantial amount with regard to her immaterial damage. This was the last drop that caused the bucket to overflow. The little toilet roll was immediately expelled from his duties and a few days later he was fired! He felt being used. Other nasty emotions were being added to this feeling. He considered himself as being misunderstood, as being let down and he felt awfully alone and sad. The life of an unemployed person gave him a very hard time. The little toilet roll got very depressed as a reason of which he began to start drinking a lot of alcohol. Once upon a night he had a dream. He saw an exquisite white angel with two little wings. "Who are you?", the little toilet roll asked. "I'm a panty liner and I have come to help you", the angel said. "I don't want to be rough anymore! I want to become well-liked and successful! Please tell me how I'll be able to change my life", the little toilet roll begged. "Look for the source of your anxieties. That's the place where the roots of your misery are hiding", the angel answered. "How will I be able to go searching for these roots?", the little toilet roll asked. "Use the trauma-meditation and you will find them", the angel said.

Epilogue

Expressing emotions

All nasty emotions, which we are hiding, avoiding and concealing for years and years in a row, are leading us towards unconscious stress in our bodies. The long-lasting stress is a cause of many physical illnesses. The sorrow, which had been saved up and bottled up during a long time, is searching a way out and eventually changes into anger. Don't try to hide your nasty emotions. Look for a safe way to express them. The trauma-meditation could be such a way.

Ask for feedback

How well do you know yourself? Ask your nearest neighbourhood for feedback. How do they look upon you? How do they judge the way you react in certain situations? You should consider the feedback as a present of which you should take advantage.

Emotions in daily life

I can imagine that you're too busy during weekday to stand still at every nasty emotion. I myself use to "park" (like a car) the nasty emotion for a while, until I've got enough time to engage myself in it. I use to make a brief remark in my notebook or in the diary of target-feelings about the nasty emotion itself and a situation which has evoked this emotion. These notes can be restricted to a minimum. For instance: Tuesday. Meeting. Got very annoyed at Marks attitude. This irritation is my target-feeling, which I'm going to heal later on during my trauma-meditation.

Earning money with your nasty emotions

Do you want to make money with the aid of your nasty emotions? It's possible. Write a book about yourself, your handling of your nasty emotions and your experience with trauma-meditations. It doesn't have to be complicated. You can classify your book into three chapters. Chapter 1. What's your current situation? Chapter 2. Your logbook of trauma-meditations. Chapter 3. How are you changed? By means of writing a book you're killing two birds with one stone. You're going to get rid of your nasty emotions and you'll be able to earn money with your book.

When your book is finished, you can publish it on Amazon (www.createspace.com).

Software and Community

We have developed software for Mindfulness Based Trauma Treatment (MBTT). This software helps you to keep track of your emotions and your progress. It also consist a logbook for trauma-meditations and target-feelings. Please visit our community website www.MindfulnessBasedTraumaTreatment.com if you want to download this software. You will need a password in order to get access to the download page. This password is 1913. Please do not share it with anyone.

You can also read about my experience with EMDR (Eye movement desensitization and reprocessing) and

Cognitive behavioral therapy on our website. This also applies to looking at the photographs of persons appearing in this book.

If you have any questions to ask or if you want to share your experience, please post them in the forum of our self-help support exchange community on www.MindfulnessBasedTraumaTreatment.com. You can also get in touch with people like yourself and even find a buddy. All of this completely anonymous. We only use nicknames.

Please be aware of the necessity, that you should always consult a healthcare professional before you start using the software and Mindfulness Based Trauma Treatment (MBTT). Your own recovery should incorporate the guidance of trauma trained professionals.

Your opinion

What's your opinion on my book? I would greatly appreciate if you post a short comment (review) on Amazon. Your review will help to reach other people who are suffering from trauma.

Glossary

Philippe-reaction – a behaviour-pattern with an emotional reaction which is being evoked by a trauma from the past. A behaviour-pattern is a repetition of the same behaviour.

Jukebox – a metaphor for the mechanism behind the association of our emotions with (traumatic) events from the past and the present.

Logbook of trauma-meditation – a diary for keeping count of experiences from trauma-meditations.

Diary of target-feelings – a notebook for writing down nasty emotions in the course of one week. The purpose of this is to use these nasty emotions as target-feelings during trauma-meditations in due time.

Trauma-meditation – a mindfulness based meditation for healing traumas from the past. The trauma-meditation consists of the take-off procedure, trauma-hunting and trauma-programming.

Mindfulness based trauma treatment – a mindfulness based process of trauma-healing; a (self)treatment, which consists of trauma-meditations and writing-therapy (logbook of trauma-meditations).

Target-feeling – a nasty emotion, on which you concentrate yourself in (during) the trauma-meditation.

Mousetrap – the waiting period during which you are concentrating yourself on the target-feeling with the purpose to track down an associated memory.

Take-off procedure – a procedure during which you are bringing yourself in a light sleep with the purpose to reach "the state of mind", which is giving you access to your unconsciousness.

Trauma-hunting – hunting traumatic events from the past in the subconsciousness.

Trauma-programming – reliving traumatic experiences during the trauma-meditation, in which the nasty emotions are being expressed and replaced by positive emotions.

Trauma-paradise – a self-created virtual location in the mind, where you are feeling safe, carefree and happy.

References

1. Francine Shapiro. Eye Movement Desensitization and Reprocessing: Basic Principles, Protocols, and Procedures. 2001

2. George Victor, Hitler: The Pathology of Evil. 1999

3. Simon Sebag Montefiore, Stalin's youth years, from rebel to red czar. 2007

4. Steven Seagal
   http://en.wikipedia.org/wiki/Steven_Seagal

5. Buddhism in Kalmykia
   http://en.wikipedia.org/wiki/Kalmykia

Notes

....
....
....
....
....
....
....
....
....
....
....
....
....
....
....
....
....
....
....
....
....
....
....
....
....
....
....
....
....
....
....

www.ingramcontent.com/pod-product-compliance
Lightning Source LLC
Chambersburg PA
CBHW070633290526
45790CB00001B/88